ANGOLA IN MY
HEART

MARGARET SKEA

ANGOLA IN MY HEART

The Story of Ruth Hadley

MARGARET SKEA

ECHOES INTERNATIONAL

Together with joy

Copyright © Echoes International 2023

Author: Margaret Skea

All rights reserved. No part of this book may be reproduced or used in any manner without written permission of the copyright owner except for the use of quotations in a book review.

First edition January 2023

Book and cover design by Luz Design
Chapter illustrations: Kristina Abbott

Grateful thanks go to the many people who contributed to the writing of this book, both in the UK and in Angola.

© All images used with permission

Lyrics used with permission: *Yet Not I But Through Christ in Me*, Michael Farren, Jonny Robinson, Rich Thompson

© 2018 Integrity's Alleluia! Music (SESAC), Farren Love And War (SESAC), CityAlight Music (APRA) (all adm. at IntegratedRights.com)

ISBN 978-1-9169058-3-2

Printed in Great Britain by Bell and Bain Ltd, Glasgow

Contents

Map of Angola

Foreword

'Choose you this day whom you will serve.'[1]

When God calls, there is always a choice. For Ruth Hadley that call came during her time as a student at Royal Holloway College. It came as the call of God often comes, at an unexpected time and in an unexpected manner. As part of her history course, she had to choose a topic for a dissertation. In her words:

> *'I wanted a subject our college didn't offer, so that I could get a free trip up to one of the central London colleges – and thus a night in London. I hit on a topic offered by the School of Oriental and African Studies called* Christianity in Africa south of the Sahara from 1850.*'*

Accepting the Professor's suggestion to study the method and impact of early brethren missionaries turned out to be a life-changing experience. As she put it:

> *'The lives of those young men and women who went out to Central Angola at the end of the nineteenth century challenged me both in their commitment to a purpose, however difficult, and in their walk with the Lord. Increasingly I saw the shallowness of my own life.'*

As she researched, she became interested in the Chokwe tribe in north-eastern Angola and prayed that the Lord would send other folk to help in the work. Her words again:

> *'The more I prayed, the more I heard an internal voice saying,*
> 'What about you?'*

She could have ignored the challenge, and indeed tried hard to do so for a period, for there were other 'pulls' on her life, other pathways she could follow. Perhaps the strongest alternative was sport.

---

1   Joshua ch 24 v 15

Growing up as the only girl in a family of boys had given her the drive to beat her brothers no matter what, and to excel at everything she tried. And excel she did, playing tennis at county level (one claim to fame was that she had played against Sue Barker) and hockey at both club and county level and in her early twenties was under consideration for the England international squad, with the expectation that she would, at some stage, play for her country.

A career in sport was an enticing prospect and one that she recognised would bring great personal satisfaction. In contrast, answering God's call to go as a missionary to Angola would mean enormous sacrifices – she would have to leave behind the possibility of a rewarding career, a comfortable life, her family, her many friends, not least the friendship of a young man, which, if allowed to develop, could lead to marriage and children of her own.

Over the next few months, as she wrestled with this call, God demolished her excuses one by one, until finally she responded:

'Here I am, send me.'

It was to be another four years before Ruth arrived in Angola to begin a lifetime of service to the people of Angola and particularly the Chokwe tribe that had first caught her attention.

If you are a person of faith, perhaps you think a missionary is some sort of 'super-Christian'. If you aren't, perhaps you'll consider her crazy to have done what she did. But Ruth was neither super-spiritual nor crazy. What follows is, on the one hand, a very human story, a patchwork of courage and comradeship, and of humour and hardship. There were moments of joy and satisfaction and also of heartache and tears. She faced many challenges and frustrations and periods of danger and disappointment, as well as struggles with environment and culture, with mistakes and self-doubt. No one, missionary or otherwise, gets it right all the time. But above all it is a testament to what God can do with and in a life, however imperfect, surrendered to Him.

I am grateful to the many people, both in the UK and in Angola, who gave freely of their time to share their memories of Ruth and their personal photographs, who took me to key places in Chokweland and around Luanda and introduced me to many of the people who had worked with her.

All of them played a part in the production of this book, enabling me to build a picture of her life and work. Where appropriate, I have used her own words, taken from letters or from relayed conversations.

There is a hymn that seems to me to characterise Ruth Hadley and the legacy she left, not only to the Chokwes, whom she came to respect and love, but also to many others in Angola and around the world. I believe it is how Ruth herself would have summed up her life's work. It is reproduced in full on the following page, with kind permission from the authors – CityAlight. And although it wasn't written until 2018, the final line of each stanza could have been Ruth's motto: 'Yet not I, but through Christ in me.'

Although it is impossible to cover everything that she did, and all that happened to and through her during her thirty-four and a half years of service in Angola, I trust that, as you read, you will get a glimpse of Ruth and more especially of the God she loved and lived to serve.

Yet Not I but Through Christ in Me

(Song by CityAlight)

What gift of grace is Jesus my redeemer
There is no more for heaven now to give
He is my joy, my righteousness, and freedom
My steadfast love, my deep and boundless peace

To this I hold, my hope is only Jesus
For my live is wholly bound to His
Oh, how strange and divine, I can sing 'All is mine'
Yet not I, but through Christ in me

The night is dark but I am not forsaken
For by my side, the Saviour He will stay
I labour on in weakness and rejoicing
For in my need, His power is displayed

To this I hold, my Shepherd will defend me
Through the deepest valley He will lead
Oh, the night has been won, and I shall overcome
Yet not I, but through Christ in me

No fate I dread, I know I am forgiven
The future sure, the price it has been paid
For Jesus bled and suffered for my pardon
And He was raised to overthrow the grave

To this I hold, my sin has been defeated
Jesus now and ever is my plea
Oh, the chains are released, I can sing 'I am free'
Yet not I, but through Christ in me

With every breath I long to follow Jesus
For He has said that He will bring me home
And day by day I know He will renew me
Until I stand with joy before the throne

To this I hold, my hope is only Jesus
All the glory evermore to Him
When the race is complete, still my lips shall repeat
Yet not I, but through Christ in me

Reproduced by kind permission: Integrity Music

Timeline

Ruth Joy Hadley

DOB
2nd February 1956

1967
Became a Christian.

1969
Reaffirmed her commitment to Christ through baptism in the swimming pool at Chy an Goon camp.

1981
Went to Portugal for intensive language study to learn Portuguese.

1982
Went out to Biula mission station in Lunda Sul province, Angola, to begin her missionary service.

1984
Was forced by the encroaching civil war to move from Biula to Luanda (rejecting the advice from the British Embassy to return to the UK).

1989
Relocated to Saurimo, a government held town in Lunda Sul province.

1993
Once again the British Embassy advised a return to the UK, instead Ruth wrote a letter absolving the UK government of any responsibility for her as she had made the decision to remain. She stayed in Saurimo for the remainder of her service.

December 2016

Ruth found a lump in her breast and came home to the UK for medical assessment.

January 2017

Ruth was diagnosed with an aggressive cancer, which failed to respond to treatment.

June 2017

Ruth moved to the Mount Edgecumbe Hospice in St Austell.

July 2017

Ruth passed peacefully into the presence of her Lord on the 19th July, surrounded by her family. Óbitos (wakes) were held for her in various places in Angola.

August 2017

Her funeral was held on 11th August in St Austell, Cornwall. A private graveside service was followed by a Thanksgiving service attended by several hundred people.

Chapter One

'Chimwe chifuchi kusuku'
'A far country'

Christmas Eve, 2016

When Ruth landed at Heathrow airport on Christmas Eve 2016, on the last British Airways flight out of Luanda before the holidays, it was, though she didn't know it, also the last time she would make that journey. She had come home several times before for a medical diagnosis that wasn't available to her in Angola, but the need for it, just three months after her last health check in the UK, was unexpected and unsettling. The eight-and-a-half-hour flight was direct and uneventful, with, unusually, no delays. It was an overnight flight, and when, like most people, she found it difficult to sleep, memories of her arrival and early days in Angola, over thirty-four years before, crowded in on her, each one as vivid as if it were yesterday.

Angola, 1982: Arrival

Ruth travelled to Biula mission station in Lunda Sul province of north-eastern Angola in June 1982, to a country already racked by internal tensions and faction fighting. Independence from Portuguese colonial rule had not brought stability. Instead of taking three days, as it would now, the journey had taken two and a half weeks, the first and easiest leg the four-and-a-half-hour drive with her father from Cornwall to Heathrow, followed by the overnight flight to Luanda. She had to wait in the cramped missionary flat in Luanda for almost a week for an internal flight, which brought into stark contrast the life she had left behind and the life she was beginning. There was a further week's wait for her main luggage to arrive in Saurimo via a cargo plane, and finally a four-hour, one hundred and eighty-kilometre drive to Biula. The whole process illustrated just how different travel in Angola would be.

She had been glad to have company on that long journey. Another couple, from Northern Ireland, were travelling to Biula as guests of George and Ena Wiseman – the resident missionaries. It was a short 'prospecting' visit, to see if they felt God leading them to join the mission team. Ruth, however, was going to stay. She had never met Eric and Margaret McCaughren before, though they had corresponded during her time of language study in Portugal. In typical Ruth fashion, she met them at the check-in desk at Heathrow strung about with a multitude of extra bits of hand baggage – way beyond what was allowed – as well as a guitar slung across her back. With the guitar, her long hair and long, patterned skirt, she could have been mistaken for a hippy, rather than someone about to embark on years of missionary service. And to the McCaughren's amazement she managed to get all her additional bits and pieces through check-in free of charge. It was the first indication of her ability to cajole and manage officialdom that proved an essential skill in Angola.

The flight from Heathrow was busy, the arrival in Luanda challenging. The airport was hot and crowded, a mêlée of total confusion. At the immigration desk Eric and Margaret couldn't understand what was said, but they saw there was some problem with their passports. Immigration in any communist country can be nerve-wracking at best and frightening at worst, and they found it intimidating. Not Ruth. They had been advised to travel on Southern Irish rather than British passports, due to the state of relations between Britain and Angola. It turned out to be poor advice, as it raised a red flag for the immigration officer, who recognised the discrepancy between their passports and their home address. Ruth, thinking on her feet and already proficient in Portuguese, stepped in to say that the United Kingdom consisted of four parts – England, Ireland, Scotland and Wales, and the crisis was over.

Luanda city was chaotic, packed full of people who had fled the fighting in the interior. Shanty dwellings of plastic and scrag-ends of timber and corrugated iron spread out in every direction. The noise was constant, the sheer number of people oppressive. Charlie and Betty Shorten, who had been missionaries in Angola for thirty-five years, welcomed them into their small two-bedroomed flat. It was the only available accommodation for all mission workers passing through the capital. Although hotels existed, booking was reserved to the communist party, their officials, and others who were either welcomed by the government or who could 'pull strings'. The flat was on the top floor of an apartment block that would have been every building control officer's nightmare in Britain, condemned as uninhabitable and likely scheduled for demolition. There were lift shafts, but no working lifts. The corridors were damp, dirty and smelly, with electricity wires stretched loosely along the tops of the walls and dangling in loops. Running water reached only to the third floor and had to be carried in basins and buckets up the remaining four flights. It was a far cry from the elegant and comfortable Woodbridge School accommodation that Ruth had left.

Inside the flat, however, it was an oasis of calm, the Shortens making every effort to make it seem like a little bit of 'home'. Despite their lovely welcome, the lack of running water, the minimal cooking facilities and the stack of mattresses piled up, ready to be spread out on the floors when required, were a reminder, if any should be needed, that this was not the UK. Forty years later, visiting that same block, it remains a symbol of how little has changed in the living standards of the ordinary people, the view from the living room window still of shanty dwellings stretching as far as the eye can see. In shocking contrast, the glittering dome of the impressive new parliament building, more suited to Washington DC than Luanda, dominates the skyline in the background.

The booking office of Angolan Airways – in Portuguese TAAG, nicknamed by those travelling into the interior as 'Think Again About Going' – was even more crammed than the airport. Booking gave no guarantee of travel; there was no automatic connection between having a ticket and getting on a plane, and no clear indication if a flight would go, or when. Chaos reigned, and when the office was so tightly packed that no one else could get in, those at the back attempted to scramble up to walk over everyone else's shoulders, complete with their luggage, to get to the front of the queue.

When they finally got on a flight, their personal luggage travelled with them, but the 200-litre lidded metal drums had to go by cargo plane. The McCaughrens' drum contained food and fragile items, such as a typewriter and parts for a generator. Ruth's two drums, as well as more food and some other items requested by George and Ena, held everything she could think of that she might need for the next few years until her first 'furlough' – a home visit intended for rest and recuperation, and a chance to let those churches and individuals who were supporting her know about the work she was doing. They had come up from Biula to Saurimo to meet them and so all five waited together in the unoccupied mission house at Camundambala, a village ten kilometres away. Thirty years later Ruth wrote about that first night: *watching the mice (large ones with bushy tails) run around the top of the walls, petrified in case they should come down while she slept.* And just as the food George and Ena had brought began to run out, the cargo plane arrived. Ena had begun to be concerned, but George had been relaxed, confident that God had it all under control. It was a lesson in trust that Ruth, in common with many missionaries, experienced many times during her years of service – for God often takes you right to the wire before providing for your need. At Luanda they had driven out to the airport in Charlie Shorten's pickup, Ruth travelling in the open back, surrounded by heaps of luggage, grateful that thus far it had survived intact, aside from a broken mirror and stolen padlocks. Collecting it at Saurimo, they drove straight onto the runway and parked under the wing of the plane to unload their baggage straight onto their own vehicle. It was one way of ensuring that nothing went 'missing' in the process. Much of it was food, for shops were government controlled. Party members received a card, which enabled them to buy supplies; without a card it was almost impossible to buy anything.

For Ruth, coming from the wild beauty of Cornwall, it was a joy to find that after the claustrophobic chaos of Luanda and the drabness of Saurimo, Biula was also beautiful, the surrounding landscape an attractive blend of red soil contrasting with the vibrant green of the trees. The mission station was an oasis of well-watered grass, shaded by elegant stems of bamboo. They stretched upwards, silhouetted against the immense skies: pale at dawn, ripening to the ochre and pink and yellow and fiery red of the sunsets. It was a welcome end to a journey that Ruth was glad she wouldn't be repeating anytime soon. It was perhaps just as well she didn't know then that in just two years, due to the encroaching war, she would have to evacuate from Biula, first to Luanda, and finally, a few years later, make the move to a permanent base in Saurimo.

The mission team at Biula consisted of George and Ena from the UK and two single ladies from Canada, Doris Pitman and Marjorie Beckwith (nicknamed Becky). All were elderly. George's primary role was to preach and teach. Ena and Becky, who were both nurses, worked in the very busy local rural hospital and ran the attached dispensary. There was also a TB clinic and a large leper village close by. Doris was a teacher, and as well as taking meetings and supporting Sunday school teachers, she did translation work and was in charge of marking the Emmaus Bible correspondence courses. They were all kept very busy and were excited to have a new and younger member of the team.

They were delighted with the food that Ruth, Eric and Margaret had brought, and it didn't take long for Ruth to understand why. Although fruit and vegetables were grown around Biula, supplies were limited and the resultant prices extortionate. A single cabbage cost the equivalent of £6–£10 sterling, and just three cabbage leaves £2. Meat of any kind was even scarcer, and even if they could have found some for sale, the prices made it almost out of reach. A chicken, however scrawny, cost £40, a duck £70 and a pig £200. The only chance the missionaries had of achieving anything remotely approaching a balanced diet was through the supplies of dried and packaged food that arrived from home. As a result of the long civil war, it was a situation that lasted through much of the period Ruth was in Angola.

Looking back to her childhood, she began to understand how growing up as the daughter of an unsalaried, itinerant evangelist was preparation for some of the privations she now shared with her missionary colleagues and with the local population. As a family they had often experienced times of real hardship, not knowing when or from where their next meal would come. She had witnessed her parent's unshakeable faith in God, and had seen the results of that faith in the gifts they received, sometimes from people they knew, often from those they didn't, exactly when they needed it. In many ways a difficult upbringing for a child, it was a lesson in 'living by faith' that encouraged her now, and reminded her that, though sometimes God would test her faith and allow her to face trials, His promise was that it would never be 'beyond what she could bear'. That promise became increasingly important as tensions in the country grew.

There were constant rumours of war, and Ruth found it hard to imagine if war did erupt how the people around them would manage to find enough food to survive.

It was the dry season, and day after day the skies were cloudless, a clear, rinsed blue. The temperature was in the high twenties, a welcome change from the cooler high teens she had left in the UK. The mornings began with a breeze, the branches of bamboo dipping and swaying, a constant background whisper to the chirruping of small birds. By afternoon the air had settled, the horizon was a shimmering haze and the scrub vegetation beyond the watered grass crackled underfoot. The anthill-mud road was baked hard, dust everywhere, inside and out. Although the days were pleasantly hot, the nights were cold, and Eric and Margaret, unprepared for the contrast, were glad of the jumpers that Betty Shorten found for them in a suitcase left in the flat. Ruth, knowing she was here to stay, had brought clothes for all seasons, so wasn't caught out by the evening drop in temperature. Later, when the first rains came, she wrote home of the explosion of colour as small flowers sprung up almost overnight. Her favourite were the ground orchids, which stood out, purple and white against the black ashes of the burnt-off scrub.

Initially, she had one small room on the end of a mud-brick mission house, which was entered from the outside. It had no ceiling, no mosquito net, and, as at Camundambala, a myriad of creatures living in the thatch above her head that were liable to fall or jump down on her at any moment. Fear of spiders in the UK is a common but mostly irrational reaction to the length of legs or the speed of movement. As a child Ruth had screamed at the sight of the tiniest spider, needing a brother or her father to rescue her. Here she was faced with what the locals called 'Jumping Jennies'. She supposed they were probably part of the grasshopper family, for their back legs resembled frogs' legs, but with their big fat bodies and their ability to move and to jump they looked and seemed more like spiders. They were amongst her worst nightmares and the size of her hand, so it didn't help much to be told they were perfectly harmless. She included a squashed one in a letter to her brother, confessing that, *'harmless or not, and armed with a shoe, I've chased and killed twenty-seven of them in my room.'* It had felt like a victory of sorts to have been able to tackle them at all, but the idea that she would ever get to the stage of ignoring them seemed remote in the extreme.

Language learning was hard going, for there was no formal mechanism for learning, apart from a grammar book written by a previous missionary that she was working through. Not being particularly good at languages at school, it had been one of the excuses she'd made to God when she first felt a missionary 'call' to Angola. She had been surprised at her own steady progress in learning Portuguese, but it at least shared common Latin roots with much of English. Chokwe was entirely different. Listening to her colleagues as they talked with the local people was initially dispiriting. She could pick out individual words, but it seemed like one in a hundred, and she found it very difficult to look ahead to when she too would be able to join in conversations and not feel so totally at sea. The children were the biggest help. Their bright, inquisitive eyes danced when she tried to speak to them, their laughter at her mistakes totally without malice. More importantly, they weren't afraid to correct her. The women were likewise fascinated by her attempts and gathered round. 'Speak!' they said, but though their amusement was equally obvious, they were less willing to openly correct her.

Helping Doris with the marking of Emmaus coursework in Portuguese was the one part of her week that felt like 'real' missionary work. It was harder to reconcile herself to the other more mundane tasks that took up quite a bit of her time while she attempted to learn Chokwe. Mixing cement and carting mud bricks was far from what she had imagined her missionary work would involve. Little did she know then that this was a helpful preparation for the many years of work to come.

At first, when verbal communication was almost impossible, she played football with the younger boys, glad she could begin to build relationships through the 'beautiful game', enjoying the relaxation and relief from her studies. This throwback to her tomboy childhood, and the endless hours of playing sport of all kinds with her brothers, now proved its value in a time and a place she could never have imagined. It was another small but significant sign that she was the right person in the right place and that God can and does make use of natural talents in his work.

The problems of language learning and creepy-crawlies and work that wasn't as fulfilling as she might have hoped weren't the only challenges she faced in her first year. Psychologists tell us that the first year of anything is stressful – be it a new job, a new location or a new home. Ruth had all of these to cope with, and, in addition, a new country, new climate, and new culture, any one of which would have been difficult to handle on its own. But there was another challenge that she found particularly hard.

Her fellow missionaries were elderly and had been on the mission field for decades. Ruth was still in her twenties and a child of the more free and easy sixties and seventies. Her job at the private school in which she had taught for three years was a responsible one, including being a 'House Mother', so she was perfectly capable of being a disciplinarian when appropriate, but nevertheless, formality and rigid routines didn't come easily to her. Nor did she see any particular value in them in this new context.

The senior missionaries' lifestyle was the same as it had been since their earliest days and they saw no reason to change. Ruth recognised their undoubted love for and commitment to the local people, but she struggled with some of their attitudes and modes of living. They were a product of colonialism, while she had grown up in a very different atmosphere. She understood the two single ladies, with whom she ate most of her meals, needed to have someone to cook for them, for they worked such long hours they had little time to spare for the preparation of food. But, while grateful for the meals, she found the habit of ringing a bell when ready to eat, so that the 'boy' scurried in with the food, and scurried away again, only to return when summoned to clear away afterwards, totally alien and more than faintly embarrassing. The hierarchical attitude that practices like this implied made her uncomfortable, for she hadn't come to Angola to be in a position of superiority to the local people but to draw alongside them, and by so doing share her faith.

In this she was part of a new breed of missionaries, when the old colonial attitudes were gradually being eroded and replaced by a new understanding of a missionary as complementary to the local Christians. Their task was to fill in where there were gaps in knowledge or experience, while equipping local Christians to increasingly take ownership of the work themselves. This new attitude was, sadly, sometimes resisted even by the locals, who often shared in the false belief of the superiority of the white person. It has become widely accepted now, though it is possible to still find occasional glimpses of the old ways. One person, when telling me about a mistake Ruth had made, expressed how surprised they'd been and how much it had meant to them when she apologised, as they hadn't expected a white person to humble themselves to that extent.

Small differences of opinion and practice can, in a close community, become magnified out of all proportion. This, too, Ruth experienced in that first difficult year. She had always loved games, whether sport or board games, but was fiercely competitive, and played to win. While this stood her in good stead when playing football with the young Angolan lads, it did not fit well with the polite games of Scrabble her fellow missionaries sometimes played in the evenings, closeted in a mission house. She found it incredibly frustrating when they helped each other to find words to put down. The cooperative spirit was, in her opinion, quite at odds with the purpose and intent of the game and destroyed any pleasure she might have got from it.

She drank tea, while the two Canadian ladies with whom she ate, drank coffee. They were very busy during the day and didn't feel the need to stop, whereas Ruth missed her afternoon 'cuppa'. Feeling she wasn't free to go into the kitchen to make tea for herself, and not wishing to ask the 'boy', she resorted to boiling water in her bedroom on a little Primus stove she'd brought out from the UK. That met her immediate need but increased a feeling of loneliness and contributed to her wondering in those early days if she'd been right to come. George and Ena were her salvation, for when they realised what she was doing, they told her to come to them at any time and they would have a cup of tea with her. Sometimes it is on such trivial issues that relationships founder, and it was a tribute to their wisdom and their concern for Ruth that they put themselves out to make her feel she belonged.

Another area of adjustment wasn't all one way. Ruth, though she wouldn't have claimed to be a musician of the quality of one of her brothers, was, nevertheless, a competent guitarist. She wanted to encourage the young people's interest in spiritual matters and felt that music would help. So, as soon as she had learned enough Chokwe to be able to sing some of the hymns, she invited teenagers to join her in the evenings in the church building to sing with her. The senior missionaries thought this wasn't entirely appropriate, not least because the guitar, as an instrument associated with pop music, seemed rather 'worldly'. We may smile at these ideas now, from the perspective of 2022, but in the early 1980s there were many, particularly elderly folk, who shared those feelings. Ruth, convinced they were out-dated and unproductive, stood up for what she was sure was the right approach. In this, it was the senior missionaries who adapted.

Although there were many periods during her service when Ruth was alone, there were others when, through circumstances, she both worked and lived with other missionary personnel. It wasn't always easy. People have different personalities, lifestyles, and approaches to their physical environment. Missionaries are just like everyone else, and however much they share the same goals, differences in perspective can present difficulties. This is especially true when the situation in which they find themselves is already physically, mentally and emotionally challenging. Sometimes the best solution may be for each person to have their own space. It shouldn't be seen as failure, but rather a pragmatic way to reduce stress and thus be more effective in working together to fulfil their primary aim.

Many years later, Ruth said if there had been the opportunity to go out for a short-term trial period, as is often the case in missionary work today, she might not have stayed the course but would instead have retreated to the familiarity of home, family and career in double-quick time. She didn't have that option, and there were various other factors that combined to provide an incentive to ride out the difficulties. The first and most important was her strong sense of the specific call of God on her life – to full-time service and to the north-eastern corner of Angola in particular. She also found she couldn't ignore the obvious needs, both practical and spiritual, she saw all around her. It wasn't just the needs of the Chokwes, though they were huge, but also those of her fellow missionaries, who, conscious of their increasing age, desperately wanted to know the work would continue when they were gone. However inadequate she felt at times, their legacy, and that of the generations of missionaries before them, inspired and encouraged her and made it impossible to run away.

Chapter Two

'Mashimbu akwo chuma chimuwika mulinga kulila hamwe no'
'Sometimes we can only weep with them.'

Cornwall, 2017

Ruth had never spent a lot of time watching TV. She hadn't grown up with one as a child and was always much more interested in outdoor activities, particularly sports of any kind. While teaching, she often spent her lunchtime break in hockey 'goal' practice – as she was the penalty flick taker for her club team she wanted to ensure she would score in a match. Her practice consisted of shooting five hundred times into one corner of the net and five hundred into the other. As she grew up, she did have some favourite programmes, and with the advent of box sets, she was able to watch them when time permitted, particularly when she was home on furlough. One series she'd always enjoyed was Dad's Army. In February 2017, BBC2 was running episodes and she sat down with her brother to watch 'The Battle of Godfrey's Cottage'. It was welcome light relief.

As I was working through the letters that Ruth sent home, in preparation for writing this book, Putin declared what he called a 'Special Military Operation' in Ukraine, which was what most of the rest of the world called a war. As the Russian army advanced and missiles began to rain down on towns and cities in the east of the country, damaging homes and infrastructure and cutting off water and food supplies, refugees began to flood westwards. They left with only what they could carry, or in the case of those whose homes had been destroyed, with almost nothing at all. The images of the impact of the war on ordinary people, the privations, the distress, the dislocation and the terror, were a vivid illustration of the situation that much of the population of Angola faced throughout their many years of war. Their problems weren't caused by an invading army but by internal political divisions tearing the country apart. *Dad's Army* it was not.

Angola: War

Early in 1983 the problems for both the missionary team and the local population at Biula multiplied as terrorist activity in the surrounding bush intensified. UNITA (National Union For The Total Independence Of Angola) were close by and very few people were willing to travel on the roads, making the already difficult food supply issues much worse. The road to Luena was still open, with government-supporting Cuban troops guarding the nearby bridge over the river Cassai, and the team at Biula felt confident to remain while the bridge was held. It allowed them access to the town to check for mail and to pick up what foodstuffs were available.

However, the political situation deteriorated rapidly, and it was no surprise when, in August, they heard of the first mine being laid on the road to Saurimo and the first fatalities as a truck was blown up. UNITA was pushing northwards and the safety of the mission at Biula depended on the success or failure of the advance. Thankful for the Cubans' presence, they built a rapport with the soldiers and made use of the unexpected opportunity to witness to them and give them gospel literature in Spanish. It was an unlikely friendship, but the soldiers were also a long way from home and appreciated friendly contact.

Growing up in Cornwall where the sea was never far away, Ruth had spent a lot of time on the beach. In her first few weeks at home, in early 2017, between tests and medical assessments, she made visits to various beaches and coastal cliffs to watch the sea. Standing on the beach at Porthluney Cove on the south Cornish coast, watching as the waves rolled in, Ruth thought of all the times in the past when she'd been swimming. Of the first few shivery minutes wading in without the benefit of a wetsuit, her arms crossed tight around her chest. And the gradual warming up once it was deep enough to launch herself forward, as long as she kept most of her body under water. They had been a far cry from one of the most memorable swims of her life.

In the middle of the hottest month of 1983, Ruth longed for a swim. When she mentioned this in conversation with the Cuban officer, he made her an offer she couldn't refuse. It proved to be a somewhat embarrassing experience and one that bemused both her colleagues and the local villagers. She had her swim in a pool in the river near the bridge, with a guard of honour of Cuban soldiers surrounding her on the banks, discharging their guns every few minutes to keep the crocodiles at bay. It was one of those bizarre, amusing, stand-out memories, a light-hearted moment in that increasingly dangerous time to share with her family and friends at home.

Although Biula was still relatively calm, the seriousness of the situation in surrounding areas was forcibly brought home to them when they regularly tuned in to the BBC World Service to hear what was happening outside of their local area. The first serious challenge to their resolve to stay came in November when they heard disturbing news. According to the bulletin, five ladies had been taken captive from the mission station at Cazombo to the north. Ruth and Doris immediately went to Luena to see if they could verify the report. At first, conflicting reports filtered through. The ladies were under house arrest at Cazombo; they were all captives of UNITA; they were on the 'long march south' to the UNITA stronghold of Huambo. The commissioner at Cazombo confirmed that the ladies weren't there, but they got first-hand evidence of what had actually happened when two of the alleged captives, Emily and Eva arrived at Biula. Nora and Marion had indeed been taken and were presumed to be walking south through the bush. Though UNITA were reputed to treat innocent captives well, the physical and health dangers of such a march – strenuous and unpleasant at any time – were multiplied in the wet season. Ruth hoped, though she couldn't get any confirmation, that the Red Cross were negotiating for their release, as one of the ladies had already been unwell before her capture and so was a serious concern.

The team at Biula, which by this stage included a young couple from Canada, Louise and Peter Daley, who had one child and another on the way, met to discuss what they should do. They could all move to Camundambala, where the visitors' house had recently been repaired, as it was further from the war zone. Ruth didn't fear for herself, but she had concerns for George and Ena because of their age and poor health, as well as for the young Canadian couple. Should George and Ena be captured and forced to go south, they might not survive the march through the bush. None of them wanted to depend on the presence of the Cubans defending the bridge, nor to over-react to the potential danger. In the end it was decided that each person should seek God's guidance for their own decision. For the time being they all remained, including the ladies from Cazombo. That was a difficult decision for them, thinking of what it meant for the locals in that area, for the hospital at Cazombo couldn't continue without missionary input.

By mid-December the situation had deteriorated further, the road to Luena churned up by the caterpillar tracks of tanks and big guns, and they were told by locals that it was very dangerous. When Ruth needed to rush a maternity patient to the clinic at Luena, she had no choice but to risk it. She took the opportunity to have lunch with the local commissioner and discuss Emily and Eva's situation. They wanted to be allowed out to Lumbala and from there to fly either to Ireland via Zambia, or to stay at Chavuma mission. Her trip was successful on three counts – she got to Luena and back safely; permission was granted for Emily and Eva to travel; and Ruth enjoyed the rare treat of a chicken and spaghetti lunch. The next day, she returned to Luena and saw Emily and Eva off to the UK, and despite the dangers on the roads she was still determined to stay at Biula. George, as the senior missionary, felt responsible for all the others, and he now insisted that the decision to go or stay should be taken collectively.

Rumours and counter-rumours abounded and it was hard to sift truth from propaganda. The government claimed that UNITA had a camp central to the three main towns in the area and were attacking in all directions. The train line was mined, as were the roads from Biula to Cazaje in the east and Luau to the north. It seemed likely that UNITA's plan was to surround Luena and Luau, and if either of those should fall then the mission group at Biula would consider moving. In the meantime, their work continued, though on a restricted level. Ruth took responsibility for the Emmaus Bible correspondence courses and a Sunday school class in a village close by. She wanted to make the most of the time, for she felt despondent that just as she was becoming more confident in Chokwe, they might all have to pull out.

Not knowing that UNITA had attacked the road, Ruth set out again for Luena, and though she passed through three military controls, she wasn't turned back. A burnt-out car at the side of the road was a sober reminder of the potential dangers of her journey. In Luena she learnt there had been three civilians in the burnt-out car, but it had been shot up because it was a military vehicle. So, when the commissioner insisted on providing an escort for her return to Biula, she had no option other than to accept. As soon as she was past the first military control, however, she put the accelerator to the floor and left the escort far behind, reckoning she was safer on her own.

The word from Cazombo was that there was nothing left of the mission station, the local people had scattered, and in their area too, many had fled the villages because of the fighting, refugees pouring into Luena from all over the Alto Zambeze.

On Christmas Eve, they received the first bit of good news, once again via the World Service. Nora and Marion, the two ladies captured at Cazombo, had been released by UNITA and flown to Heathrow. They spent Christmas Day in a hotel with missionary staff from the UK, who then saw them safely onto a flight home to Canada. They had been walking through the bush for forty-two days, much of the time waist-deep in water. It was an ever-present danger, and though George felt responsible for everyone, Ruth wrote:

> *All is well here, but increasingly precarious. I want it on record that I am totally responsible for my own actions… I am fully aware of the possibilities and dangers and daily considering my position prayerfully. As yet I feel no reason to leave. If God has called me here, he can keep me. I feel my life is no more at risk here than travelling down the M4 or M5. None of us have the desire to play the hero or martyr, nor are we made of that sort of stuff… Our desire is to be faithful and to move when He indicates.*

She was encouraged by the enthusiasm of her Sunday school class at Sasuçu, most of whom had learned Psalm 23 by heart and were now learning John chapter 3. As they were unable to read, it was a significant achievement, especially considering the constant deafening rain on the tin roof. In December in Angola, the average number of days with rain is thirty… out of thirty-one! Despite the shortages of almost everything, she was delighted to still have enough sugar left to prepare five pieces of fudge for each child. Unlike the children at the mission station, who had become used to receiving a small gift, they hadn't expected anything, and she couldn't help wondering what the reaction of British children would be if a tiny packet of fudge was the only Christmas present they received.

By January shortages had become acute, with a lack of food, fuel, medicines and even salt, and they were surrounded by large numbers of hungry people. It was unclear how long they could or should remain. Camundambala no longer seemed any safer than Biula, so there was little point in thinking of moving there. They took a day at a time but began to organise what would happen if they did have to leave, so as not to leave chaos behind. Ruth, who by this time was helping to mark the Emmaus Bible correspondence courses, was particularly concerned for that work and so planned to go to Luanda to continue from there.

Following embassy advice to leave, George and Ena left for the US in March 1984 and Louise and Peter followed to Canada in April. Though Ruth missed them, she was glad they were all safe, and especially that Louise wouldn't be delivering her baby while on a forced march south. Doris, Becky and Ruth took the heart-rending decision, in principle, to leave Biula, but hung on, living out of suitcases, ready to go at a moment's notice should it become absolutely necessary. Day by day their thoughts see-sawed between leaving and staying, especially as they expected a lull in rebel activity with the onset of the dry season, largely because they would lose the cover of thick bush.

In May UNITA did move south, removing the immediate danger. Ruth wrote home and thanked folk for their prayers, and explained that she, Doris and Becky were still at Biula and felt the presence of God with them. She wrote, '*The last of our diesel is in the vehicles, so there is no fuel for the generator and therefore no lights – which used to discourage the lions we'd sometimes heard prowling around the mission station at night.*'

With the nearest access to post at Luena, some sixty miles away, she couldn't carry on with the Emmaus work without fuel for the car, which was a particular concern. Some food parcels had come through and they were very grateful, but they were still waiting for a convoy to arrive with milk and medicines and books. They didn't want to leave until the convoy had arrived so they could ensure the distribution was left in the hands of local elders. They understood only too well that if UNITA wished to take them captive they could do so easily, and realised that unless agreement was reached between the government and the rebels before the wet season, they would have no choice but to leave.

The plight of the Angolans was heartbreaking – many were chronically ill, food was hard to find, and in their despondency and suffering, illness and death fanned the flames of fear of witchcraft. It was a low point for Ruth, realising how little she understood of their fears. Coupled with the knowledge that she might not be in Biula for very much longer, she was aware how little she could do to allay them, other than pray.

They hung on throughout the dry season, despite the disappointment of continued warfare in the area. A nearby village was attacked and seventeen people killed. The government sent several lorryloads of troops, ammunition and supplies intended to wipe out the rebel force. Instead, UNITA attacked at dawn, burning all the trucks and killing a large number of the soldiers. Word reached Biula by lunchtime and by evening the wounded began to trickle in. Two days later five more lorryloads of government troops were sent, but they fled without firing a shot, for they were mostly fourteen- to sixteen-year-old conscripts. Their age, more than anything else, brought home the horrifying realities of war. When I visited, twenty years after the end of the hostilities, men told me of how, during a church service, if they heard the sound of a vehicle, they would jump out of the church windows and run away to escape conscription. One man who had been forcibly conscripted into the FPLA (the People's Armed Forces of Liberation of Angola) recounted how he had deserted, and to avoid being caught he had joined the police force, though he'd no desire to be a policeman.

The UNITA advance and atrocities continued. A bridge on the road to Luena was blown up and a group of Catholics returning to Dala from Saurimo were attacked. The Polish priest and a Spanish nun were taken into the bush, and four of the seven Angolans with them were killed. When Dala itself was threatened and the villagers fled, Doris, Becky and Ruth made the trip to Luena for the last time: Doris and Becky to leave for Canada and Ruth to remain to sort out the Emmaus work and prepare for the transfer to Luanda. The mission was left in the hands of the local elders, but Ruth was torn. On the one hand she felt she was running away, leaving the locals to cope with the ongoing problems – the Cubans who wanted their houses and the UNITA forces who surrounded the village. On the other hand, she knew as the rains began it was time to leave.

Most of the Christians told her it wasn't safe for her to stay, but one or two challenged her: 'You tell us to trust in God. Why can't you?' She knew it was said as a result of deep disappointment, rather than a criticism, nevertheless it chimed with her own thoughts and her inner conflict. She knew also that she shouldn't rely on her 'feelings' when taking decisions of what to do, but on the promise that God was in control and knew what would best serve the work. One encouragement and confirmation that she was making the right decision to go to Luanda was that one of the Angolans involved in marking the Emmaus courses was also prepared to uproot his family and move to Luanda to help. She would have liked to be able to see further ahead than the next step, but she realised that facing uncertainties was also a lesson in trust.

As they hoped to return before too long, they left much of their stuff in store, praying it would still be there when they got back, despite the risk of theft. As she left, after only two years, Ruth had an overwhelming sense that the future, however unclear, was in God's hands. Her prayer was for peace for Angola and an end to the suffering. It was a prayer destined not to receive an answer for many years. Over the next eighteen months, that triggered a challenge to Ruth's calling and resolve.

Prior to the instant nature of email contact, when Ruth wrote home her news would be six weeks old by the time it was received. With the increasing tensions she was aware that news broadcast on the BBC might worry her family. It wasn't an unrealistic concern. On one occasion her family were listening to the BBC World Service and heard that she'd been captured by UNITA. They contacted the Foreign Office, who confirmed the report. Ruth had heard the same broadcast but had no way of letting anyone in the UK know that she wasn't in the hands of the rebels. Fortunately, one of her brothers managed to contact a mercenary, who in turn was able to make contact with UNITA and was assured they didn't have Ruth. While that was good news for her family, Ruth's parents didn't know whether to be relieved she was safe or worried that her brother had been able to find out. It was six weeks before word came from Ruth herself, confirming her safety.

On relocating to Luanda, she and Iris Floyd, who was working with Luvale-speaking refugees brought by the government from the Alto-Zambeze, lived with the Shortens in their flat, which had been Ruth's introduction to Angola. The lack of privacy was hard on them all, despite their mutual support in what remained a very uncertain situation. Stuck in Luanda, Ruth focused on the Emmaus work and helping Betty Shorten in her mission work among the Chokwes. She enjoyed working alongside an older and more experienced person and recognised it would be a useful period of learning for her, but she constantly felt the 'pull' of the interior.

Several times, in the five years that Ruth stayed in Luanda, she and Becky, who had returned to Angola from Canada and settled in Luanda for the remainder of her service, made short trips back to Lunda Sul, flying to Luena on Soviet military transport.

On the first trip, the folk in Luena felt the road was too dangerous for them to travel on to Biula, but when elders from Biula cycled down to try to persuade them to go, they needed little encouragement. Their concession to the potential danger was to delay leaving until mid-morning, so that any mines or guerrilla movements would already have been detected. The road conditions meant that a journey that should have taken one hour took four and a half. But the welcome they received made their effort worthwhile. In the few days they were able to stay, Becky saw to the hospital, while Ruth had a profitable discussion of the Emmaus work with the two Angolans who had taken it on. It was clear that peace was elusive, so decisions needed to be made for the longer term. Although emptying the store at Biula was an admission that they wouldn't be likely to be able to return to live there, it seemed the best option, especially as the local commissioner had already stolen their Land Rover, as well as other items. They decided to give away what they could to the Christians, and removed the rest for safekeeping.

On their way back to Luena they were greeted at all the villages en route. At one, the Christians lined the roadside to shake their hands and sing a hymn, at others they held meetings for the women, and all the way they were loaded with gifts of pineapples, tomatoes and even a chicken. It was intensely moving to be given so much by those who had so little. When they flew down again, this time during the rainy season, they found half of the roof of the mission house had been damaged by a mortar shell and they had to sleep in the church office. As Ruth said, '*We'd always hoped one day to have running water in the house, but water running all night through the missing roof wasn't quite what we'd had in mind.*'

The sadness and destruction was everywhere, the impact of war not just obvious on the buildings and roads, but also in the people. They were so much thinner and more poorly dressed than those in Luanda, their suffering heartbreaking. Becky was inundated with medical consultations and requests for medicines she couldn't provide, which left them with a gut-wrenching dilemma. They couldn't continue to pay staff for doing very little, and with the lack of available medicine, they needed to scale back the clinic work.

The plight of the people cemented Ruth's resolve to move back to the interior as soon as she possibly could, so she began to investigate the possibility of moving to Saurimo. It was a government-held town, which she felt was a relatively safe option.

She made the move in 1989, arriving together with Mary Stewart – who had been a medical missionary in Zambia for some years. They arrived by military plane with 300 kilogrammes of baggage. The airport at that time had an international runway, three roofless aircraft hangers, several wrecked planes and a road through a field where the available transport waited on the edge of the tarmac. Aside from Mary's much-needed medical expertise, for the first time Ruth had someone of her own age to live and work alongside and she was delighted. Mary's primary role was to run a TB and general medical clinic.

When peace was declared in 1991, Ruth was sceptical, partly because the proposed UN peacekeeping force was, in her opinion, too small, and partly because the inter-tribal fighting was so ingrained in Angolan society. She was quickly proved right, and though Saurimo wasn't constantly in the thick of the conflict, there were many 'hairy' moments. In December 1992 Ruth left for Luanda to source medicines just hours before fighting broke out in Saurimo itself, as the government troops of the MPLA (People's Movement for the Liberation of Angola) sought to drive out the small UNITA contingent in the town. For Ruth, having left at exactly the right moment was a minor miracle – a sign of God's protection.

She didn't stay long in Luanda, though, for by the 8th January 1993 the government troops had expelled UNITA completely from the town, and she immediately returned.

The evidence of the fighting was all around, and the MPLA 'victory' brought other problems. In the confusion that followed, many people were killed and there was much looting of shops and warehouses. UNITA's response to the government drive to expel them from the town resulted in successful attacks on other provincial towns and villages, so that, while the town itself was in government hands, the whole surrounding area fell to UNITA control.

This in turn resulted in a flood of hungry and needy refugees, swelling the population of Saurimo from around 8,000 to 40,000.

Throughout the war Ruth managed to maintain a neutrality that stood her in good stead. On one occasion the local rebel commander warned her that they were going on the offensive and suggested she leave town for a few days. She wasn't always forewarned, though. On another occasion when fighting broke out in the town, Ruth's house was in the line of crossfire, between the government-held hotel behind her house and the UNITA forces at the cross-roads, twenty yards from her front door. She hunkered in her passageway while the gun battle raged around her. Bullet holes pockmarking the walls of the houses served as a reminder, if any was needed, of the precarious situation in which she lived.

A soldier who repeatedly came to her house and stood outside firing his gun into the air, one day shot one of her guard dogs in his attempt to intimidate her. She refused to be intimidated by either the police or troops at any time but did not take unnecessary risks. However, when it was important to drive somewhere, she negotiated the many checkpoints without compromise. Frequently she was recognised and would be let through. If not, she would explain why she was travelling and say that if they didn't let her go on, she would report them to the commissioner of police or to the commander of the army. Both of which were true, because she was well known and respected by the authorities on both sides. When bribes were demanded she refused, but instead she offered them a tract or a New Testament.

Life in Angola was like living on a see-saw – one moment, with a new government, things seemed to be improving a little, the next, rampant inflation and looming fresh elections plunged more and more people into crisis. In theory, throughout all the years of war there was a 'peace process' ongoing, but it was very slow. Sadly, the UN presence, which was intended to help the situation, served rather to undermine the economy and add to the levels of corruption and low moral standards. That was dispiriting, and for Ruth it underlined her conviction that only the power of God in people's lives could really make a difference.

After the euphoria of yet another election, which independent observers had declared fair, the mood had changed for the worse once again. Jonas Savimbi – the leader of UNITA – had failed to win, but he claimed he had been cheated and would continue the armed struggle.

The Lunda Sul area was in splendid isolation – and each morning Ruth thanked God for the Mission Aviation Fellowship radio, which was the only way to contact the folk in Luanda. This time the advice from the Foreign Office was clear and unequivocal – all British citizens should leave. Ruth didn't want to go, and as there were no planes flying, it was impossible to get out from Saurimo anyway. By the time some weeks later when planes were flying again, she had made the decision to stay put. Within Saurimo there was only sporadic shooting, most of which seemed to be aimed into the air, though of course that didn't make it safe, as what goes up must come down somewhere! But for the time being the troubles in the surrounding villages appeared to be the work of small bands rather than an all-out offensive. She discussed the situation and the advice to leave with a mix of secular and missionary personnel from a range of countries – Bulgarian teachers and Brazilian, Portuguese, Mexican, Polish and Irish priests and nuns. They all agreed it was unlikely UNITA would take Saurimo, for the only asset it had was the airport, which, some four kilometres out of town, could be taken without reference to the town itself. The relatively flat land surrounding the town ruled out a surprise attack, though they remained under siege, with all the attendant problems for the population. Fully aware of all the risks – death, rape, and capture – all the missionaries decided to stay. Ruth kept an eye on the situation from day to day, for they were cut off by road from both Biula and Luanda, and Dala had also fallen to the rebels. Nevertheless, it was a period of relative quiet in Saurimo, though the Zairense were being hounded and beaten up on the pretext they favoured UNITA and were responsible for looting during previous fighting. It was probably true that some were, but the attacks were indiscriminate, including on Zairense who had lived in Angola for years, as well as the migrant diamond hunters who abounded in the Saurimo area.

1993 heralded the beginning of what would be another nine years of war, to add to the thirty already suffered by the people, first in the War of Independence and then the following civil war. Outside agencies continued to attempt to broker peace, and several times a treaty was signed, but it never held. It was at this point, eleven years after first coming to Angola, that Ruth reaffirmed her allegiance to God and to the Chokwes. She wrote home to explain her decision to stay against all the advice. Her words 'This people will be my people' were an echo of the Ruth of the Old Testament, who, though a Moabitess, chose to leave her own land to go to live among the people of Israel. Ruth's desire was to fully integrate herself into the Chokwe culture and language and thus earn the right to share her faith and knowledge of Christ as her Saviour and Lord with them. She was conscious of God's presence with her and was sure He was saying 'Stay' when human reason said 'Go'. That didn't mean she wasn't afraid, nor unaware of the stress it placed on her family at home. And it wasn't simple bravado, for she had spent a lot of time praying and thinking about the situation and her decision hadn't been taken lightly.

She gave three main reasons why she had determined to stay. The first was that she had no clear conviction that God wanted her to leave. The second was the contribution she knew she could make in terms of the humanitarian aid required. And the third, her desire to stand with the Chokwes in adversity, and thus show them by her actions that faith in God wasn't just for the 'good times'. She couldn't see any distinction between running away when life gets tough and running to the witch doctor when difficulties arrive, and she knew the Chokwes certainly didn't. Their words – 'You're white and can go home to your own country and to your doctors when you are ill. Your society isn't based on jealousy and witchcraft as ours is, so you can't understand the dangers we face. We could trust God as you do in your society, it is different here' – convinced her she must stand with them in their adversity to prove it was possible to trust God even in the worst of circumstances. Because of the embassy advice, and recognising their sense of responsibility, Ruth wrote a formal letter exonerating them for her decision to stay.

Hurt and confused by the renewed outbreak of fighting, some of the Christians were meeting in small groups for an hour every day to pray for peace and once a week spent an entire night in prayer. They asked 'Are we more sinful than other nations? Why did God give us peace only for it to be quickly snatched away?' The truth, of course, was that it wasn't God bringing war upon them, but rather evil men that were causing the pain and suffering. But Ruth found it hard to explain why God didn't miraculously protect them from it.

While some prayed, others were caught up in the hatred and turmoil. It was one of many heartbreaking moments for Ruth when a lady in the church stood up and confessed she split a young man's head open with an axe when she saw him beside her field because she suspected him of being UNITA. In another church the elders berated the young men for a lack of enthusiasm for military training, while at a meeting between the government and church leaders, the elders promised to do everything they could to encourage their people to take up arms. She imagined that similar pressures were being put on churches and church leaders in UNITA-held territory.

As I write this the news reports are full of the situation in Afghanistan and the plight of the people there. This was the kind of situation that Ruth saw every day. We see Afghanistan or Syria or Ukraine – wherever the current crisis is taking place – on our TV screen, but Angola's war has been often called the 'forgotten' war and rarely made front page news. It was no less horrific for that, and it impacted on every aspect of both physical and spiritual life. It was thought to be the most land-mined country in the world, and the number of amputees was huge.

While I was visiting the places where Ruth worked, I was privileged to meet some members of a 'de-mining' team. Six days a week they surveyed the ground inch by inch, searching for mines which could then be detonated in controlled explosions. They had no prior maps and chose areas to survey based on reports from locals of places where someone had lost a limb. The charity they worked for had been doing this for over twenty years and knew they were nowhere near finished. The map they had plotted of the small area they were currently working in showed 972 mines, most about two feet apart.

In the autumn of 1998, there were attempts at reconciliation, despite the UN mediator dying in a plane crash. The people were tired of war but felt like pawns in the hands of the leaders, and the Christians wondered if God was punishing them. They regularly repented of their nation's sin in prayer meetings, but still peace didn't come. They didn't blame God, but rather their nation.

It was incredibly hard for Ruth to see the terrible situation of the people. Just outside Saurimo there was a new refugee camp holding around 6,000 refugees. The conditions there were dreadful and something urgently needed to be done before the rains came. The Christians in the town were doing what they could, collecting food and clothes to take out to the camp, sharing what little they had with those in even greater need. By this time her own situation and that of fellow missionaries was very little better, and they were desperate for a container with food and aid to arrive from the UK. At Camundambala, Brian and Debbie Howden, a missionary couple who had come to Angola with their two young sons, were very short of food, and so Ruth decided to go down to Luanda to try to see if there were any supplies there that could be shifted inland.

As she reflected on the past year, she wrote of how much the situation in the country had deteriorated. At the beginning of the year they'd been travelling freely by road even to Luanda – though it had been a long and arduous journey. But when the peace process collapsed for the umpteenth time, they'd returned to restricted movement, new war victims, thousands of refugees and demands for help that she simply didn't have the resources to meet. In the towns, which were without access to the villages that usually supplied the food, prices had soared and lack of food was a problem for not only refugees but also the townsfolk. Everyone was in despair, even those with government jobs, as salaries hadn't been paid for up to ten months. The head of the medical post in Saurimo came to Ruth to say he hadn't eaten for two days and was too weak to work. The situation was as bad as it had ever been. About fifty kilometres away there was a barbaric attack on the mother of one of Ruth's workers, her arms all but hacked off, and all that could be done for her was to amputate both of them.

Deaths and injuries from mines, mortars and bullets became a regular occurrence once again. The young men lost their dreams of education and feared an army call-up. She could give no guarantees of physical safety but could only point the Christians to a time in the future when there would be no more tears. The fighting had now moved towards the north-west, leaving Saurimo relatively quiet, but there had been an attack on the road to the south of it and thirty-five people killed – so it was by no means a safe haven. Meanwhile, the people in Bié, Malange and Luena were starving and it was almost impossible to reach them with any aid. The Angolan government claimed to have driven UNITA back, but the population feared counter-attacks and expected UNITA to continue a guerrilla war, the road to peace little nearer than before.

January 2001 was the twenty-fifth anniversary of Angolan independence and liberty from Portuguese control. It was the end of the War of Independence, but it hadn't proved to be liberation. First there'd been a controlling communist government, then an attempt at a transition to a market economy. But all twenty-five years had been dominated by war in one form or another. It still affected large tracts of the country, with every city full of displaced people. Those who once had owned their own homes and fields were living in grass huts in camps, dependent on the World Food Programme handouts. Even in the camps it was a struggle to find enough to eat. When Ruth managed to go down to Luena she visited an orphanage. Here she found a group of twenty-five orphans who were the remnants of a government attack on a UNITA camp. No women or young people had survived, and all the babies that were in their mother's arms also died. Though the children were highly traumatised, and only spoke Umbundu, the churches in Luena were doing their best to look after them. It was a very obvious and heartbreaking reminder of what war had done to the country and the people. She sent a poignant message home. *'Sometimes we can only weep with them.'*

It was hard to see how in human terms these children could recover from such trauma, yet she clung onto the fact that God cared deeply for each one of them, and however helpless she felt, He was able to heal even in these most terrible of circumstances.

After a short period of successful attacks on UNITA bases by government forces, it looked as if, finally, there might be some move towards 'peace'. It was hard to know what this might mean for the country long term. With money from diamonds UNITA would still be capable of waging a guerrilla war for some considerable time to come. But the people needed peace after all the years of war and constant suffering. It was yet another false dawn. In the first six months of 2001 increased military activity had driven more and more people into the towns and the camps that had sprung up around them. There were now six large refugee camps around Saurimo. When Ruth visited them, on the one hand she was encouraged to find that, as most people were illiterate, the Christians had built somewhere they could meet each morning to hear a communal Bible reading and pray together. On the other hand, she found it hard not to despair of the civil conflict ever coming to an end.

The end, when it came, was dramatic and unexpected.

Ruth was sitting at her desk, the generator in the back yard droning away, as once again Saurimo was without electricity, when she heard a repeated shout 'The assassin's dead, the assassin's dead.' Her first thought was that someone had met with the rough justice that was so much part of Angolan life, but when the cries increased and the car horns started tooting, their lights playing across the sky, she realised it was something much bigger than an ordinary criminal. At first few people believed it, until a couple of days later when Savimbi's body was paraded on national TV for everyone to see. For some it was the best news ever, their joy uncontained; for some it brought sadness that his undoubted talents and abilities had been lost in a quest for power and finally ended in a forsaken spot in the bush south of Luena. Even some of those who were relieved he was dead still spoke with respect of his contribution to multiparty government and the victory of capitalism over communism.

The question on everyone's lips following Savimbi's death and the signing of a peace accord was 'What now?' The needs were horrific. Displaced people came out of the bush with nothing and as thin as rakes. For Ruth and other missionaries it was a time of soul-searching. They had taken clothing sent out by Medical Missionary News to two camps and were going to another in a few days, but it seemed like a drop in the ocean. There was help from various NGOs, but too little, and for too few. Any help that could be provided for the immediate needs would be good, as long as it could be supervised, for it would be unwise to throw money at the situation without accountability. In Zambia, help had been provided in two camps, and their basic refugee kit comprised soap, a tarpaulin, which was a large sheet of blue plastic to make a temporary shelter, blankets, a galvanised basin, a pot, four exercise books and one pen and two pencils, a chitenge (a large piece of cloth worn like a sarong), a mosquito net and a Bible.

Replicating and distributing the kits was a complex process. While many of the items could be bought in Luanda, some needed to be purchased in South Africa and freighted up. Mosquito nets could be obtained from a factory in Tanzania, but the logistics of transport were a problem. Additional items that would be useful might need to come from the UK. The kits could be assembled in Luanda by volunteers and transported to Saurimo, Bié and Luena, with the cost and transport funded by various agencies, but a national coordinating body was needed. The plan was to have a local team of Christians at each distribution centre who would be responsible for receiving and distributing the kits. Food aid was also essential.

Alongside the urgent needs, both Angolan church leaders and government authorities pleaded with them to provide longer-term aid, rebuilding clinics and schools. Aware that wasn't their primary commission, which remained to 'go and make disciples'[2] they wrestled with the twin questions – how could

---

2   Matthew ch 28 v 19

you convince an Angolan to leave behind witchcraft practices if no medical alternative was available, and how effectively could you teach the Bible to those who couldn't read? It was clear that in order to fulfil their spiritual commission, they needed to continue to meet practical needs. For Ruth, a mix of humanitarian aid, literacy and schools work dominated much of her last fourteen years of service.

Rebuilding the country was a priority, and the government and political parties began to work on a new constitution to prepare the country for a new round of elections. Some of the Angolan political leaders had been taught in mission schools many years earlier and Ruth asked people to pray that they would remember what they'd been taught, respond to God's call for personal salvation, and so govern with honesty and equity. Foreign businesses came in, keen to stake their claim. Oil companies and diamond companies looked to protect their assets. New shops and businesses opened on an almost daily basis in Luanda, the shelves filling with every commodity imaginable. Roads to the provinces opened up, allowing some of the wealth enjoyed in Luanda to trickle through. And at first some of the Angolan Christians were caught up in the euphoria of peace. It was exciting to be able to help those who had been stuck in government-held towns as they rushed to the UNITA camps with messages of reconciliation and gifts of clothing and other goods from containers sent from the UK. Exciting also to encourage them as they planned and undertook trips to isolated rural areas to preach the word of God to Christians cut off for so long.

Disappointingly, some were caught up in the promise of easy money and relief from hardship and fought for a stake in the lucrative markets. Saddest of all were those who remained dazed and unable to look ahead. They struggled with their losses, grieved for relatives who didn't survive to see peace, and continued to eke out a meagre existence in their camps or their villages, wondering what had been the point of it all.

The peace has held, but, twenty years on, some aspects of Angolan life remain very much as they were in 2002. One aspect was travel.

Chapter Three

'Yuma yize napalikile'
'Quite an experience.'

Cornwall, 2017

In Ruth's first few weeks at home in January 2017, before she began to suffer the effects of her chemotherapy, she was able to drive herself about. She had a Citroen C3 which was perfectly suitable for the narrow, tarmacked Cornish roads, and for the distances she was travelling, but which, in comparison to the vehicles she drove in Angola, felt a little bit like a 'go-kart', and in her brother's words, 'She drove it like one.'

Angola: Travel

When Ruth first arrived in Angola she knew the road conditions, even between Luanda and the provincial capitals, wouldn't be like driving on the M4, but nevertheless the poor quality of the road from Saurimo to Biula was still a shock. Travelling to outlying villages on dust tracks winding through fields or uncultivated bush was something else again. At the tail end of the rainy season, when the humidity was dropping and the tracks were beginning to dry out, Ruth, desperate for a level of independence, used her bicycle to go out to nearby villages to practise her Chokwe and to look for possibilities for work among women and children, which had always been her vision.

Negotiating the deeply rutted sandy tracks on a bicycle wasn't quite like riding on the Cornish lanes at home, but it was a new skill she was determined to master. Many people who knew Ruth testified she had never been short on determination. It was a facet of her character that stood her in good stead many times at home, and especially in the years she spent in Angola.

By 1983 road travel was risky and the planes that were still flying no longer had space for mail because of more pressing needs, leaving Ruth and the others increasingly cut off from the outside world. When the tensions erupted into full-scale war, the impact on travel of any sort was devastating. It was no longer possible to drive even between major towns, and travel by plane was restricted to either hitching a lift (usually at a price, though occasionally free) on cargo planes carrying aid, or on military transport, neither of which were particularly comfortable or followed any kind of timetable. Word of space on a military plane usually came at about an hour's notice, with the consequent scramble to get to the airport on time. The frustrations, and ultimately the dangers of such travel, were brought home to Ruth very clearly when, as part of her evacuation process in 1984, she managed to arrange for space on a Russian military plane for herself and a Land Rover to fly down to Luanda. But when she arrived at the airport the pilot refused to allow her or the car on the flight. That in itself wasn't surprising, for she had quickly become used to the fact that nothing was guaranteed in Angola until it actually happened, but she was upset and frustrated and in tears wondered why God would leave her alone in Luena in a steadily worsening situation. A few days later she learned that the plane had been shot down and all on board killed. Some may see that as a 'lucky' escape, Ruth saw it as a sign that God was watching over her every move, and that He still had work for her to do in Angola.

Between 1984 and 2002, during the short periods of supposed 'peace', it was technically possible to travel by road. She made a second visit to Biula, once again driven from Luena by an Angolan elder in his car. Burnt-out vehicles, some with the soldiers or civilians who died in them still inside, and the occasional tank, littered the roadsides, a stark reminder that Angola was still a country at war with itself. The elder's vehicle was a hazard in itself – it had bald tyres, had to be pushed to start, none of the instrument panels worked, and the brakes and steering left a lot to be desired. Sitting in the back Ruth watched the ground go past through holes in the floor. Mobbed by the villagers, Ruth thought the car might be flattened, but their welcome and the joy with which the villagers received the medicines she'd brought were ample compensation for the dangers of the journey.

Shortly after Ruth's relocation to Saurimo in 1989, she'd hoped to get her Land Rover flown up, for the diamond mine company had a Hercules, but the cost was prohibitive. As it wasn't safe for a vehicle to attempt the nine-hundred and forty-five-kilometre journey across country alone, Moises Dias, a Christian driver, volunteered to bring it, travelling in a convoy of more than forty vehicles. The danger was clearly illustrated when the convoy was attacked, but miraculously, Ruth's Land Rover and its driver survived, despite a bullet passing through the window frame and becoming embedded in the seat belt mechanism. Sadly, however, most of the convoy was destroyed. Ruth was thankful for her Land Rover's safe arrival, complete with bullet holes to remind her of the miracle every time she looked at it. She was heartbroken at what the destruction of the remainder of the convoy meant for Saurimo, for it had been bringing food and essential medical supplies for the town, which was bursting with refugees who had fled from the fighting in the bush. Because of the increased UNITA activity in the area, it was unlikely there would be another attempt in the near future.

Three years later, early in 1992, when once again the roads were 'open', Ruth and Mary drove down to Luanda with the intention of arranging for goods from the latest container of aid to be transported inland. In a typical Ruth understatement, she described the journey as '*Quite an experience.*' Bridges which were destroyed in the fighting had been temporarily replaced with wobbly wooden planks, and the roads were cratered with mine holes. They had hoped that the tarmac might have survived intact on the road between Malange and Luanda, for the fighting hadn't been so severe in that area. But any hopes of being able to drive at a reasonable speed were dashed, for the road had so many potholes it was necessary to drive the whole way in second gear. Unmetalled sections of road had patches of deep mud, the ruts made by army vehicles so deep that they scraped the bottom of the Land Rover. The non-stop drive took them twenty hours, from 6.00 am to 2.00 am the following day, the one saving grace that the rain stayed off, for the windscreen of the Land Rover had been stolen two weeks earlier.

One ton of goods they took back with them in two Land Rovers, with Mary, Ruth and Margaret McCaughren sharing the driving of the two vehicles. Another ton they got on a Mission Aviation Fellowship flight, and 500 kilogrammes of medicines, wheelchairs, bicycles and blankets were transport-ed free of charge via UNAVEM (United Nations Angola Verification Mission) – the UN group overseeing the peace process. It was a repeat of Ruth's pow-ers of persuasion, first evidenced at Heathrow airport, which she exercised many times in her thirty-five years – in her dealings with government, with organisations, with security forces, and with individuals – all to good effect.

Their journey back inland was even more hair-raising than the trip down to Luanda had been. On the second day they came upon a truck stuck in the mud and blocking the road, so they attempted to go up the banking to get around it. They also got stuck, but passengers from the truck finally got them out by pushing, lifting, digging and shoving. The road at that point was in very bad condition, the Land Rovers rolling from side to side and in and out of huge potholes, with every possibility that they could end up with the front wheels in a hole and the rear of the vehicle in mid-air.

After the journey down, they'd decided that travelling in the dark wasn't the most sensible of courses, especially for a group of women travelling on their own. So, they aimed to stop at a village where they knew there were some Christians and thus would be assured of a welcome, somewhere to sleep and a measure of safety. At dusk they enquired how far it was to the village they hoped to reach that night, and were told it was still another fifteen kilometres. The road was supposedly 'good', so they carried on, but after another twenty-five kilometres they asked again and this time were told it was twenty-five kilometres away. Common sense dictated they stop at the next village regardless of whether there were any Christians there or not. It turned out to be a village of the Bangala tribe, who at least understood Chokwe, so Ruth, by now fluent, could communicate with them. There was no church and they'd never heard of Jesus, so Ruth and the others held an impromptu meeting. People love to sing, so they began by teaching simple Chokwe choruses, then shared the good news about Jesus. Ruth emphasised that what she was saying came from 'God's' book and was thrilled when, as they were leaving, the villagers asked to keep 'God's book' so that they could learn more. The following morning they discovered they had stopped just three kilometres short of the village that had been their target. It was yet an-other sign for Ruth that God was in control even in the smallest things – if they had kept going just a little further, the Bangalas wouldn't have had the chance to hear the gospel.

The next stretch of road was a classic example of the impact of war. They were warned it was still heavily mined, so they had to bypass it by going off-road down a steep hill to drive along the riverbank instead. It wasn't the easiest driving, even in daylight, but they were grateful both for the warning and the off-road capabilities of Land Rovers. Both Ruth and Mary were noted for their driving, handling the difficult conditions with confidence, fearlessness and speed – sometimes to the detriment of the condition of the vehicles. In typical Ruth fashion, she joked of '*Taking up rally driving when I retire from missionary work.*' She thought it would be a 'piece of cake' compared to the road conditions she travelled on during most of her time in Angola.

By this time Ruth and Mary had two Land Rovers, which over the years doubled as people carriers and transport for all manner of things, from building materials such as bags of concrete and corrugated iron roofing sheets, to humanitarian aid, including food and clothing and household items such as pots and pans. Although they were useful, their capacity was limited, and the problem of large-scale transportation of humanitarian aid and Bibles remained. The commercial cost of a single truckload of goods from Luanda to Saurimo in 1992 was around $5,000 and had to be paid in cash due to the volatile state of the Angolan economy. Hiring a lorry and a driver was marginally cheaper at $4,000, but still not economic. One cause of the increasingly inflated prices was that the UN required trucks for their use and were happy to pay exorbitant prices. The solution, from a mission point of view, was to expand their own range of vehicles to include a second-hand truck. The initial cost was substantial, but it was worth it, both to save money in the longer term and to provide the flexibility to transport goods wherever and whenever they were needed.

By 1998, the Land Rovers were nine and ten years old respectively, which, given the condition of the Angolan roads, probably equated to nearer to thirty years of wear and tear. Ruth had been intending to put some money aside towards another vehicle, for they were both beginning to show their age. But every time she thought of doing so, some other more immediate need had cropped up – for medicines, for getting the containers of aid released from the port, for buying cement for a building project and so on. The mnemonic JOY – Jesus first, others second, yourself last – was a hallmark of Ruth's service. As the condition of her vehicles didn't matter to the authorities in Angola, however inconvenient it was for her personally to have them continually breaking down, she continued to limp them along. The problems seemed never-ending. Each time the mechanic fitted one part he broke another. The only Land Rover dealer had shut down, due to UK sanctions against UNITA, so new parts were only obtainable on the black market. To send parts from the UK required an export licence, for Land Rovers were considered military vehicles. It took a minimum of six to eight weeks and a lot of red tape, most of which was impossible to fulfil. On the UK side the DTI required a signed and dated statement from the person responsible for the vehicle that it would only be used in government-held areas. It needed to be hard copy – not a fax – on headed paper, and stating the person's position and work. It had to be submitted with an accurate and complete list of parts. Hardly surprising that the only real option was for the mechanic to scrabble around scrapyards searching for parts.

In the previous year alone, Ruth had spent £1,500 on parts and labour but was no further forward. Even so, she found it hard to determine whether it would be 'nice' to have a new vehicle, or if it was an absolute necessity. However, three breakdowns in quick succession, one of which wasn't just inconvenient but potentially dangerous, happening as it did at night, emphasised the dangers for her as a single female breaking down in the bush, and convinced her to move a reliable vehicle up her priority list. However urgent the need, she wasn't in a position to buy a new vehicle herself, but God's timing is perfect, and shortly afterwards she learnt that a vehicle had been bought for her in the UK and would be sent out in the next available container.

A reliable vehicle was something to look forward to, especially as conflict had broken out again in most areas and attacks on the roads had become commonplace once again. While she waited for it to arrive, a bus was attacked on a nearby main road and several of the passengers killed. It was a warning to Ruth that for the time being she shouldn't attempt to travel too far afield. Which, as her old Land Rover continued to have a serious wheel wobble, and the new one hadn't yet arrived, wasn't altogether a bad thing. It was, however, a disappointing curtailment of her work and ministry, particularly the distribution of Bibles and hymn books, and a serious blow to the churches in the outlying villages, as they were now almost cut off from Saurimo.

After peace finally came in 2002, the mood in the country was optimistic. However, the legacy of war and the impact on travel continued, and despite her new car, most of her journeys were still less than ten kilometres outside the town. In Lunda Sul UNITA had destroyed thirty major or strategic bridges, including the one over the River Cassai at Biula, as well as thirty-eight more minor ones. It wasn't until 2005 that it became possible, in principle, to travel much longer distances, but the practicalities, particularly the condition of the roads, remained problematic.

The town of Luena was a minimum of a four-hour drive south in the dry season, stretching to eight hours in the rainy season. The folk there were crying out for help, as were the people at Biula, but the road was so bad, even in good weather, that it hammered the vehicles. In many parts it was a toss-up which was better – to stay on what remained of the tarmac and attempt to negotiate the enormous holes, or to drive through the deep sand that lined the sides of the road. The Chinese were supposed to be rebuilding the roads, but in Ruth's opinion their attempts at repair had made them worse. They had enlarged small holes and as a temporary measure had filled them with mud. In the rains and when trucks went through, it spilled out and turned the road into a quagmire, significantly increasing the driving time to Biula and Luma.

Seventeen years on I had the 'privilege' of experiencing that road at first hand. In many places it had almost completely collapsed, and though it stretches straight to the horizon for mile after mile, it might as well be a roller-coaster in terms of the driving conditions, the depth and scale of the holes and the potential for damage to vehicles. It was a testament to Ruth's commitment to the Chokwe people, her determination, and her driving skill, that, regardless of the road conditions, she made that journey whenever she could.

Breakdowns and accidents were an ongoing hazard, and repairs became a major issue, for following the declaration of peace, the cost of labour in Angola had skyrocketed. Ruth was capable of carrying out many maintenance tasks on the Land Rovers, though not all the larger jobs, but the mission truck was a different matter altogether. Following an accident and the loss of some of the goods, getting the truck back on the road was a priority. However, the money required for the anticipated work was likely to be almost more than it was worth. Ruth only knew one local mechanic with sufficient know-how to fix it, so she was in no position to try to negotiate a better deal. The ideal solution, in the short term, was to get a volunteer mechanic out from the UK, provided the truck was mendable and they could get the parts. She knew that while the condition of the roads remained dire, she would continue to need practical help, but in the meantime, she asked the folk at home to pray for safety in travel not only for herself, but also the Angolans who worked alongside her.

Over her remaining years, from 2003 to 2016, she gradually built up a fleet of vehicles for mission use. She needed extra drivers and paid for professional driving lessons for Angolans she considered had the potential to be good drivers. Good or not, it didn't stop her commenting on or correcting their driving style when she thought it appropriate, though she didn't appreciate it if they tried to comment on hers! She had a lifelong love affair with Land Rovers and they remained the workhorses, transporting both goods and people, but she was delighted when in 2005 a Toyota Land Cruiser was gifted to the Saurimo brethren, to enable gifted men to go out to the villages to preach. It freed up her vehicles for taking young Angolan men out to the villages and refugee camps surrounding Saurimo, to teach in the newly established Sunday schools, and for bringing in women who lived in more remote villages for women's 'camps' and avoided the potential for additional stress on her vehicles that multiple drivers could produce.

As well as the mission vehicles, Ruth, perhaps remembering her own early forays out to the villages, decided to use a gift she received from the UK to buy Raleigh 'Third World' bicycles – which were a bit like old butcher's bikes with large baskets on the front. They served a dual function: on the one hand they enabled both men and women to go out to the villages to teach – the men focusing on the men and the women on women and children. At the same time, it gave them the means of transporting their garden produce to town to sell, and thus helped them to support their families and to buy other essentials. She bought one special gift for an elderly man who had served God faithfully throughout the communist era at great personal cost. Having encouraged people to go to church on a Sunday instead of attending communist rallies, the authorities penalised him, using him as forced labour, ordering him to build ten houses for the elderly without any help. He did it without complaint, but also, refusing to be cowed, continued to preach about Jesus. Ruth was thrilled to see his tearful reaction when she presented him with a motorbike, both as a recognition of his past service, and to enable him to continue.

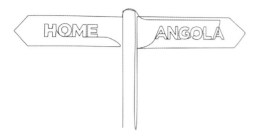

Chapter Four

'Muya ni musala'
'Go or stay?'

Christmas 2016

Ruth hadn't expected to be home for Christmas in 2016, for she'd only been back in Angola for six weeks. She woke on Christmas morning, determined not to allow any thought of the medical assessments to come to spoil the day for her family. Lying quietly, without the need to be up and bustling about, she thought of the many Christmases she'd spent in Angola, sometimes on her own, sometimes with company, but always busy. The preparations for her first Christmas at Biula had in some ways been reminiscent of home, but also very different.

Angola, 1982

Christmas was coming, but at Biula the goose was definitely not getting fat. In contrast to a chilly Cornwall, December in Angola was uncomfortably hot and humid, with almost constant cloud cover and rain most days. There was little wind, and the days themselves, though dull, were the longest of the year.

At home, Ruth would have been involved in helping to organise youth events and Sunday school services and parties. In Biula too, the preparations for the children's carol service were a priority. Ruth, despite the limitations of her Chokwe, helped as much as she could. Anyone who has ever helped to prepare children for a carol service or a nativity play will recognise the frantic rehearsals, the rush to get everything ready, the constant hope that 'It'll be all right on the night'. In Biula it wasn't held at some convenient time in order not to disrupt what has increasingly in the Western world become the focus of Christmas – the food, the gifts, the family time, the excesses and overindulgence. Instead, in this communist country, where the holiday was not called Christmas, for that would have been a recognition of religious significance, but rather 'Family Day', the children's service was held on the afternoon of Christmas Day itself. It was an attempt to emphasise that Christmas should be all about Jesus. With the main Christmas service in the morning, it made for a rather rushed lunch, though the missionary 'family' did enjoy the rare treat of a small rooster together.

The morning service was well attended, but the hall was crammed for the children's service, with standing room only inside. Those who couldn't get in crushed at the door and windows, craning to see the children perform with the same enthusiasm of parents and grandparents worldwide. It was a great opportunity to share the message of the gospel with folk who might not normally attend church, and after the children had done their part, one of the Angolan elders told the Christmas story to the adults. Ruth still understood little of what was said, but the audience was clearly attentive.

In the UK the children taking part would receive yet another selection box to add to their stash of more chocolate than they could healthily consume. Here, the Sunday school children were also excited at the prospect of sweets. But there were no selection boxes to buy and the little parcels of home-made sweets they distributed brought the contrast to home sharply into focus.

It wasn't until the evening that there was time for Ruth and the others to relax and to open their gifts to each other. Their pleasure was tempered by the fact that Charlie and Betty Shorten were unable to join them from Luanda and they weren't sure why. George and Ena had driven to Saurimo to collect them, only to find that the plane they should have come in on hadn't flown; and although they met the next one also, they weren't on it either. It was disappointing, but not an unusual occurrence. Wartime Christmases were even more challenging. Angolans traditionally eat chicken on Christmas Day, but in the long war years it was out of reach for the majority of the population in the interior.

The few evangelical missionaries were thinly spread across the country and rarely managed to all get together. Charlie and Betty were in Luanda in the west, Iris Floyd was at Cavungo, five ladies were at Cazombo, to the east, and the small team that Ruth was part of was in between, at Biula. Of these, only one person, Patricia Steen, was of a similar age to Ruth and also at a similar stage. The distances were so huge and the road conditions so poor that travel, other than within their own local areas, was usually for a very specific reason, making the times when they did meet up very special. All goods that were imported came in via Luanda and were brought up country either as air freight, or, in the case of a vehicle, generally driven to where it was needed. When a Land Rover arrived in Luanda for Iris, it was a welcome opportunity. Charlie and Betty drove it as far as Biula, and Patricia accompanied Iris when she came to collect it. The time they spent together was lovely for them all, but especially so for Ruth and Patricia – the first chance either of them had to talk through their problems in adapting and settling in, and to encourage each other in the knowledge that their experience was shared.

Cornwall, 2017

A few days after Ruth's diagnosis of an aggressive breast cancer in January 2017 she went to visit Wayne Bury. He and his wife had been responsible for sending out Ruth's prayer letters and through the years had been a constant support. Ruth Bury had also been Ruth's best friend and 'partner in crime' through all the years she'd attended the Morthoe youth camps, both as camper and as an officer. She had died of cancer some years earlier, and Wayne was now battling cancer himself, which wasn't the outcome any of them would have imagined back in the camp days. It was a bittersweet visit, triggering many memories of the 'ups and downs' she had shared with them over the years. They, more than perhaps anybody else, had been with her in spirit in times of excitement and of encouragement, of personal crises and despondency. They had laughed at her humorous stories, sympathised with her difficulties and prayed her through challenging and frustrating times. One of the most difficult years of her entire service had been 1986.

Angola 1986: Decision time

Aside from the sense of 'limbo' shared by the other missionaries, following their forced move from Biula, at that time on the 'front line' of hostilities, 1986 was a period of personal crisis. As problems multiplied, Ruth found it hard to know whether it was God halting her work, and she'd made a huge mistake in coming in the first place, or Satan putting obstacles in her way. She had been lent a Land Rover by a missionary who was currently out of the country, only for it to be stolen. The following week the Shorten's Land Rover was also stolen, and when it turned up a week later, Ruth's bag, keys and her precious residence permit were gone. They had taken the person who'd stolen it to the police, and Ruth had her first real taste of life in a land without justice. The only way to get any redress would have been through bribery, threats, or friends in high places. Unwilling to resort to corrupt means and sickened by them, they withdrew the case.

The loss of the vehicle meant she couldn't get out to the church at Viana which had become the main focus of her missionary work, and she wasn't sure what her next step should be. Go back inland? Find other work in the city? Focus on the Emmaus work? Upset and confused, even her 'quiet times' – when she tried to read her Bible and pray – gave her no comfort or direction, and she became depressed. Despite letters and phone calls of support, and folk assuring her of their special times of prayer for her, she couldn't rise above the feelings of uncertainty. And with them a sense of personal failure, of allowing Satan to have the victory.

She visited Saurimo, to see if it would be possible to go back there, for she still felt Chokweland was where she should be. That too was a disappointment. When she went to one of the churches they refused to allow her to take communion, which was both incredibly hurtful and caused her to question once again should she go home or stay? All the privations, all the difficulties she had faced since coming to Angola, seemed worth nothing to the Saurimo elders. It was only the welcome she received from many of the women that gave her the grit and the grace to hang on.

She hadn't had a chance to see her family for four years, and so it was high time she had a home visit. She intended her furlough to be six months, but in the event, she was in the UK for nine and found it incredibly hard when she went back. In Angola it was almost impossible to find any time to rest or relax, and she missed her family and the fun and fellowship she had enjoyed while at home. An old desire resurfaced. Sometimes it is in the smallest details that the hardest challenges come, and for Ruth her love for sport, and the seeming impossibility of being able to participate in it in Angola, was a fresh challenge to her commitment, just as it had been when she'd first heard God's call. And trivial as it seemed, she had an intense longing to play tennis.

There was another, even more challenging, issue. After six weeks and several unsuccessful visits to the immigration office to collect her residence permit, she found her name up on a wall in the office with a label attached – 'Return to her own country'. It was a shock, and on top of her own doubts about coming back, it made her once again question whether she should be there at all. She couldn't help feeling, though she wouldn't have admitted it openly to any of the other missionaries, that it was an escape route, a way of leaving without it seeming to be her choice. But when she shared the problem with the women at the church she'd been attending since coming to Luanda, they wept and prayed with her, and two of the church elders contacted a captain they knew in the security police to find out what the problem was. The news was not good. Ruth was accused of being a saboteur and trying to set up two identities. The problem had arisen because of her move from Biula and her request to transfer her file from Saurimo to Luanda. When she attempted to explain, she was kept waiting in the office for three hours, which felt much, much longer, and was then told to fill out yet another form and pay the fee all over again. She was promised her case would be reviewed, and eventually it was. The authorities claimed it had been nothing more than a bureaucratic 'hiccup' (in a communist country, 'errors' did not occur) and she was free to stay, though the card itself took many more weeks to arrive.

What began as a serious worry became a tremendous source of encouragement. The spontaneous display of love and concern on the part of the Chokwes, and their willingness to call special prayer meetings, to travel in the twenty-kilometres daily to visit her, and especially to tackle the authorities on her behalf, was humbling. And when the folk at Saurimo, seventeen hours away, also sent an elder down to Luanda to offer assistance, Ruth was ashamed of her reluctance to stay.

As an antidote to all the stress, her longing to play tennis was fulfilled in a most unexpected way. It reassured her that God cared about all aspects of her life, down to the last detail, and reinforced her sense of being in the right place, despite the difficulties. On the Queen's birthday every year, the British

Embassy in Luanda held a reception for UK nationals. Had Ruth been in Saurimo at the time, it would have been irrelevant, but as she was in Luanda, she was invited. She was a reluctant guest, for she wasn't into 'posh' clothes or fancy events. But it would have been discourteous to refuse. When the ambassador asked what she most missed about home, she said tennis, and she was immediately invited to come and play with him. Whether or not he regretted the invitation when he found how good a player she was, I don't know, but it was a lifeline to Ruth, and gave her the emotional and physical outlet she needed to enable her to cope with the challenges of that difficult year. Which was just as well, for it wasn't long until she faced another challenge.

Just as it seemed her problem with a visa was resolved, her presence in the country was threatened in a different, less personal way. 1986 was also a difficult year for the Angolan churches. As a result of the communist ethos of the government, religion was only tolerated provided it could be contained. All churches were designated as belonging to the Department of Culture, and so everything that was done had to first have permission from them. Initially the only impact on independent churches was in relation to requests for visas, but a new ruling meant the department could decide which churches should be allowed to function. All others would be declared illegal. There were a multitude of churches and sects in Angola, and two lists were published – those that were 'recognised' and those that were 'illegal'. The latter were closed down and members threatened with imprisonment if they met. Most of the evangelical churches, including the independent churches that Ruth was associated with, didn't appear on either list. Thus they were in an uncomfortable 'limbo' while they awaited a decision on their future. If they were declared illegal, the missionaries would be removed and the Angolan evangelical Christians under threat. There appeared to be a political aspect to the decisions already made, as the majority of the 'recognised' churches were in the west of the country within the tribes that formed the majority in government. The independent church fellowships had never been involved politically, but it was still a matter of concern.

The main barrier to the recognition of the independent churches was that they had no formal organisation. Some provincial governments had closed individual churches, but in Luanda they were allowed to remain open until a final decision was made. It was increasingly clear that some form of organisation acceptable to the government was a must, while at the same time the intent was to find a way to preserve the independence of local congregations in terms of their day-to-day running. For the first time in the history of these churches there would be salaried posts, with a minimum requirement of a national president, secretary, and treasurer.

Initially the debates that followed raised issues and problems which re-opened old wounds and drove a wedge between missionary personnel and some of the Angolan nationals. Caught in the crossfire, Ruth could under-stand some of the issues, and sympathise with the Angolan point of view, but others were historical issues she knew nothing about. The latter stemmed from colonialism, from perceived racism, from a sense of oppression, of hoarded resources, and from power politics influenced by the constant propa-ganda of the party, who asked them what the church had given to the people. The main demand was simple – 'Now that the "Mission" doesn't exist, but only the church, the missionaries should hand over all the funds they receive from abroad and be paid in local currency.'

It was yet another challenge to her determination to stay. She was under pressure, near to exhaustion, and alone in the flat in Luanda. Without Charlie and Betty, who were temporarily in Canada for health reasons, and therefore with no one with whom to talk things through, she felt inadequate to cope. Her initial reaction was understandable and very human. If it was just her money they wanted they could take it and she would go home, where she could relax, laugh, live well and enjoy friendships again. Thinking rationally, she knew that the difficulties were identical to those experienced in other African countries, which had gone through similar political and cultural changes. And her own recent experience of the outpouring of support over her visa problems showed it was only the view of a vociferous minority. Nevertheless, she found it hard to exercise patience and tact or to know how to respond. She wrote home, sharing openly her feelings and asking *'for prayer, that I might be able to administer God's love in a world where death, hunger, bribery, corruption and injustice abound; a world devoid even of human kindness.'*

It was a long-running saga to achieve recognition for the churches and a strain on both the local Christians and the missionaries. There were also worrying signs of what recognition might mean, as other churches had been asked to speak out on political matters in line with the Angolan government position. A structure was established, with a secretariado in Luanda, officially in charge of the 'Brethren Church in Angola' (IEIA) as it was labelled, and local secretariados in all the provinces. A conference was held every four years thereafter at which the national secretariado was elected. Over the years, secretariados came and went and there were many periods of happy fellowship. Inevitably, there were also periods when difficulties arose between the national secretariado and the missionaries, and between the national and local secretariados. It wasn't always easy to strike the right balance between organisation and autonomy, which rested on the spiritual calibre of those elected to positions of authority.

Almost thirty-five years on, though Angola is technically a democracy, total freedom of worship isn't guaranteed and so some concerns remain. For Ruth there were also other more practical issues to come to terms with, including her living conditions.

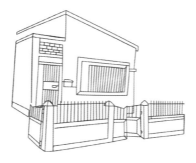

Chapter Five

'Kuinapema kuyishi tututu'
'Clean and bug-free'

Cornwall, 2017

The lounge in Ruth's house at St Austell had a large south-facing picture window. Even in the winter, if the sun was shining, it poured in from mid-morning to mid-afternoon brightening up the day. It overlooked the town, the view uninterrupted by the burglar bars which had become essential for security in Angola. Enjoying the clear expanse of glass, and the light, she thought back to her house in Saurimo, which had been her base since 1989.

Angola: Living conditions

When she moved up to Saurimo with Mary, the house had three rooms, a bathroom, a small kitchen, and a pantry with some industrial-style metal shelving. It was also clean and bug-free – a definite bonus. It did not have reliable electricity, piped water, or proper sanitation. She constantly had to remind herself of positives. Because of the war the missionaries had left the mission station and were living among the people. For Ruth that represented a much healthier, and potentially more effective, way of carrying out mission work, avoiding the previous colonial divisions. Life for the folk around them was a daily cycle of survival. The whole day could be spent in looking for

enough food to provide one meal for a family. Sickness touched every family
and every week they had a funeral to attend of a relative or a church member.
They shared the practical problems of those they were living among – carting
all their water, cooking on charcoal, attempting to grow some vegetables in a
small garden, cleaning, and trying to find food or fuel to buy. This provided
additional opportunities to share their faith, but limited the time available.
For even for themselves, with at least the possibility of some supplies from
outside, however intermittent, daily living took up so much of their time
and energy. And when the spiritual needs of those they lived among were so
obvious, it was hard not to be able to respond to them all.

It had been at Christmas in 1998, sixteen years after coming to Angola,
when she finally got running water. It hadn't been a planned improvement.
Eric and Margaret McCaughren had come up to Saurimo for Christmas.
When they ended up stranded, due to the rebels bringing down two planes
near Huambo, which in turn led to the suspension of all flights, Eric decided to make good use of his unexpectedly extended stay. Ruth still had to
buy her water in 200-litre drums at the roadside, but instead of carting it
in buckets and storing it in her unplumbed-in bath, it was pumped up to a
tank at roof height and then gravity-fed into the house system. He had also
installed a flushing toilet, which she reported as 'the best Christmas present
ever.' She'd been pleased, not just for herself, but for the many people she often
accommodated. Six months later the water system in the house was finished
and she finally had hot water. In a nod to holiday horror stories, one of her
visitors joked that she could now offer her house as a timeshare. Her ability
to laugh about her living conditions was a vital part of dealing with them.
When she finally came home in December 2016, she left a house with enormous cracks in the walls, caused in 2014 by pile-driving for the foundations
of a multistorey hotel building behind it. The authorities, as her landlord,
wouldn't agree, either to fix the problems, or to let her buy the house so she
could fix them herself. So, two years on they remained, with six-inch strips
of tape stuck across them at intervals, a symbol of the bureaucratic madness
the population still lived under.

Cornwall, 2017

*The central heating boiler in her house was playing up, despite the engineer
coming out three times in two weeks and fitting a new pump. Ruth's brother*

was desperate for it to be fixed before she started her chemotherapy. In her latter years Ruth's furloughs had usually been a month in the main Angolan school holidays, which fell between November and February. She'd spent the first week wearing her coat inside until she'd acclimatised (a little). This time, the effects of the treatment would mean for a lot of the time she would be confined to the house and likely needing to rest. As a result, he suspected she'd feel the cold even more than she normally did. Fortunately, it turned out to be a simple thermostat issue, for during February and March, as her illness progressed, the central heating did become increasingly important. Each time she heard the boiler click on, it reminded her of the power supply issues which had dogged her in Saurimo throughout the war years and beyond.

It wasn't the heat that she'd required there, but rather the power to run lights, and essentials such as her fridge and freezer, her photocopier for Bible study and Sunday school worksheets, and her laptop – the main (and least expensive, though not cheap) means of communication for much of the war years, both within the country and to family and church at home. Saurimo only had one small generator operating, due to lack of fuel, so much of the city was entirely without electricity. Ruth's house was in an area which did get some supply, but only for a couple of hours each night. She still had some diesel for her own generator, but hoarded it for emergencies in case she couldn't get any more. For several months in late 1997 and into 1998 there was no electricity in Saurimo at all, and Ruth's generator was also broken and needed a part from England. Briefly, in mid-February the city electricity was restored and they had more than ever before. Ruth wasn't sure whether it was to help them forget the long period without any power, or whether it would be more permanent. But she used it while it was there, for it gave her an opportunity to catch up on emails – in lieu of the non-existent postal service. It wasn't until 2004 that her home church managed to winkle the information out of her that the elderly generator she used to supply the house when the town electricity wasn't available (which was often) was inadequate to meet the needs of a house, and more importantly was also falling apart, spewing out black fumes – not guaranteed to endear her to her neighbours. It needed to be replaced.

The church agreed to price one in the UK and check out transport and port costs and Ruth would price one in Luanda. They'd go with the cheaper option. Neither turned out to be cheap!

The customs costs were huge – the generator itself cost £4,900 to buy in the UK, but when port costs were added (at both ends) it came to £7,900. Nevertheless, as her home church knew it was essential, one was purchased and sent out. It was, in Ruth's words, 'a red-letter day' when it finally arrived in late September 2004. It arrived in Saurimo on the back of a lorry, but the problem was how to get it from the lorry on the street to the cement pad behind her house using only manpower. Ruth described how they did it, beginning with one of her many flashes of humour:

> 'We left it on the lorry on Sunday, so I could have time to study Stonehenge…'

She continued:

> 'Step one – use the crane from another lorry to lift it onto the back of the Land Rover – having removed the back top.
>
> Step 2 – reverse the Land Rover down the side of the house towards the cement base.
>
> Step 3 – with fourteen people, a spare wheel and three old tyres and a lot of heaving and puffing, get it onto the tyres. Then, while the men heaved, I pulled out one tyre at a time and ran round to put it in front, repeating the action again and again until it arrived at its final resting place.
>
> Step 4 – lots of clapping and rejoicing.'

It would have been nice to report that she was able to use it immediately, but it wasn't that simple. It needed to be commissioned for use – but as Ruth had a women's camp coming up, and couldn't put aside the time for sorting the generator, it sat gleaming (but useless) in her backyard while she turned off everything else in the house – fridge, freezer, lights, etc. – in order to do the photocopying for the camp. It was, as always, a matter of priorities, and she promised herself that once the camp was over, commissioning the generator would move right to the top of her list.

In the first month after Ruth's diagnosis and before the chemotherapy had begun to 'bite', many people came to visit her. Although her brother was living with her, he was working so wasn't able to be around for much of the day. She loved having company and it was always an excuse for a cup of tea and a chance to talk about Angola, which was still very much on her heart. As her treatment progressed, the numbers calling in tailed off, but she was still glad to see folk. She left the door unlocked so they could come straight in.

There were many periods over the twenty-seven years that Ruth lived in Saurimo when Ruth was on her own, particularly when Mary was away. It was at these times that visitors became especially important to Ruth, not only for the practical expertise they brought, such as the MAF mechanic who was able to fix the wheel of her car after it had been off the road for a year, but also as an antidote to the 'aloneness' she sometimes felt. In 1998 she returned from furlough accompanied by a couple from her home church, Bill and Helen Evans, who had come out to help her. It was a culture shock for them, but they turned out to be a tremendous help, painting the inside of her house – something she never had time to do herself – distributing food to the TB patients, and organising the medicine store, as well as Bill doing some preaching (with Ruth translating). In their company we also see some of the fun-loving side to Ruth's character. She had a little stock of plastic spiders she could place in a visitor's bed, but in Bill's case it was a wooden snake she put in his bed and thoroughly enjoyed his reaction. It was also lovely for her to have constant, congenial company, especially as the political situation was deteriorating around her. There were other moments which were in retrospect humorous. Bill's driving style might have been learnt from Ruth and there were times when she had to extricate him from the authorities. On one occasion he did a three-point turn in the Landrover and the police having spotted him, told him the manoeuvre was illegal and tried to fine him 2,000 kwanzas. Ruth told the police that it was legal in England and he was let off. On another occasion he was told he been caught speeding by a speed trap and was to be fined 5,000 kwanzas! Ruth headed out to see the alleged speed trap and found it was a) not connected and b) facing the wrong way. Amusing as it was, it was also yet another sign of the culture of corruption. For the three months while Bill and Helen were with her Ruth didn't have to think about preparing food or cooking, and it was a welcome break to have someone else do it for her. She really missed them when they left. Following the death of Savimbi and the prospect of a real peace, Ruth looked forward to a visit from her brother and mother – the first family visit in the twenty years she had been in Angola. It was her mother's only visit, as the conditions proved very hard for her, but two of her brothers and her sister-in-law visited again.

Sometimes it's possible to read between the lines as to how Ruth was feeling by the words and tone of her letters – when she said things like '*plodding along*' it's easy to see that she was tired and perhaps despondent. At other times when she was expecting visitors, particularly men who could do practical work, it was apparent that, strong and capable as she was, able to get down and often under her vehicles to work on them, there were some things she struggled with, so she was very grateful to have outside help. She often wrote of looking forward to visits and of the '*umpteen jobs lined up*' ranging from the installation or repair of water systems, to major work on her Land Rovers.

Often as Ruth writes of traumatic events, she makes light of them, dealing with stressful experiences through humour. In 1998, at the end of a week of tensions and rumours about the deteriorating situation, Brian Howden had come into Saurimo, leaving his wife and two young boys at home at Camundambala. When he got back he found them in tears, as they had been threatened, but they weren't sure whether it had been troops or police. Ruth wrote a letter to the governor and went to see him. She was then sent to the general. Eventually they got the military police and went out to Camundambala with them. By that time, of course, there was no one to be seen. She arranged for someone to go out to sleep with Brian and Debbie that night, but went ahead with Bill Evans, who was visiting at the time, to see if everything was okay. A drunken soldier, who was devoted to Ruth because he believed she'd saved his life when he took thirty-seven bullets during the conflict in Saurimo, turned up. His shouting seemed to have been the cause of the whole upset. He fell at Ruth's feet in his drunken stupor asking why they'd called the military police as he'd never harm any of the missionaries who had saved his life. He claimed he had been shouting they had nothing to worry about because if UNITA came he'd fire his gun and save them! Not knowing who he was or able to understand what he was saying, it had been very frightening for Debbie. He wanted to stay the night because the white man was scared, but as Ruth didn't think it a good idea, she bundled him and his equally drunk friend into the Land Rover to take them back to town.

Halfway there she lost power, and when they got out to try to push the car she discovered the axle had come out and the back wheel was about three feet wide of the car body. It was 7.00 pm on an Angolan moonless night, and as she couldn't send the drunks for help, she and Bill walked the four kilometres back to Camundambala, Bill leading and managing to stumble into every hole and bush along the way.

When they got back to the car and got it jacked up and the wheel shoved on sufficiently to get it off the road, Ruth set off again in Brian's car to take the drunks into town. One got out when they arrived, the other refused, so Ruth took him to the army barracks to ask them to get him off. At the gate the guard panicked and pointed his gun at Ruth and Bill, but she managed to get them to understand what she wanted. Her throwaway final remark was, '*Bill was by this time under the seat, or would have been if I'd had one – it had been stolen long ago!*' She finished by saying, '*Incidents like this shouldn't give rise to needless concern as the city is relatively stable and safe.*' It's clear the important word here was 'relatively', as nowhere in this area where UNITA controlled much of the bush outside of the towns was safe in absolute terms.

When Ruth was away from home for a period, she ensured that someone looked after the house in her absence, particularly at night. On one occasion while Ruth and Mary were visiting another town for a few days, they left an Angolan friend in charge. One evening he woke to find that thieves had broken into the generator house and the chicken pens and had stolen chickens and fuel. They returned two days later, and alerted by the guard dogs barking, he fired his shotgun into the air to try to scare them off. They turned their guns on him, so he fired again, intending to hit one of them in the leg, but the thief ducked and so took the shot in the abdomen and died. At dawn he called the police, but instead of attempting to find the other thieves, they arrested him and put him in prison. Despite Ruth's best efforts on his behalf, he was still there two months later. As a result, she resolved, however vulnerable it made them, not to keep a gun in the house.

It was rare for Ruth to mention any personal danger, though she did write in a letter home that the bath was useful to lie in, to provide a measure of protection while a gun battle between UNITA and government forces raged around her house. One lunchtime, however, she suffered a targeted attack which she admitted left her bruised and shaken.

She was crossing the road outside her house when she heard her name called out. She half turned, and a man who had taken to spending hours just standing there, hit her on the back of the head with a rock, and then, as she parried with her arm, hit her arm twice before she could wrest the rock out of his hand. As he ran to get another rock, she ran into the shop and he then smashed the windscreen of her car. At that point some passers-by and the guard from one of the shops managed to restrain him and she and they took him to the police. At first the police weren't interested, saying he was mad, therefore not their responsibility, but Ruth insisted on leaving him with them anyway. She was shocked and sore and had a severe headache, though she joked her ponytail had protected her a little. It was the first time the man had shown aggression, but it was difficult to realise that somebody wanted to do her harm, which could have been serious, so she was grateful for everyone's help. For a short time she took more care about locking her door and looked up and down the street before coming out, but a few months later she was back to functioning as normal, though her raised awareness remained.

Paperwork was vital in Angola and it was illegal to travel without the appropriate documents. Even in peacetime, losing documents (or having them stolen) was a logistical nightmare. On one occasion Ruth had her car loaded ready to go to Lubango for a conference, when her bag was snatched. It contained all her documents – passport, residence card, UK driving licence, etc., plus a lot of money for the trip. Problem one – the police didn't work in the afternoons, so she couldn't report the theft. Problem two – without her residence card she couldn't travel, so she needed to go to immigration to get special permission. Problem three – if her passport wasn't found, all the documents required to get a replacement would have to be sent to South Africa as the embassy in Luanda didn't do passports any more. The new passport would come from the UK by DHL, and although the war was over at this stage, it could still take six weeks. She hoped the bag would be dumped and she would at least get the documents back. That didn't happen, but miraculously (after spending a day in police and immigration offices) she got a document to say she could travel to the conference. She was extremely relieved when, four days later, she heard that some children had found her passport and residence card and handed them in – saving her a lot of hassle.

The issue of visas and resident permits for missionaries was often a concern. A letter of invitation was required in order to be allowed into the country, and visas had to be renewed on a regular basis. Initially, when Ruth wanted to leave the country for a home visit, she needed an exit visa, which was also time limited. If she was away for longer than the allotted time, it meant reapplying for a visa on her return. Sometimes Ruth and the others found it hard to know if the problems they faced in this regard were simply due to bureaucracy or were due to opposition to the missionaries, even sometimes from those whom they expected to be supportive. In 1997 Brian and Debbie Howden were stuck in Luanda for four months making frequent and prolonged visits to immigration before they received their resident's permits. It was a worrying time for them and for Ruth, and in a very human reaction she confessed that it '*isn't easy to cling onto a belief that God is sovereign, when everything seems to be against you*'. Yet time and time again throughout Ruth's service she found that when she most felt discouraged, God would provide some encouragement and a reminder to trust Him.

The year after Brian and Debbie's residency problems, Ruth was granted a residency card. It was lifetime residency so she no longer needed to reapply and there wouldn't be restrictions placed on the length of time she was in or out of the country. It came at a time when she was also facing disappointment regarding a prospective missionary she had hoped would be coming to Angola but who had decided to go to another country instead. Once again it was a much-needed confirmation that *she* was in the right place, however difficult the circumstances might seem. And a timely reminder that she shouldn't focus on what she wanted God to ask someone else to do, but only what she should be doing herself.

Chapter Six

'Mikanda ya ulemu munji yize alile kuli tumbi'
'Letters are too precious a commodity to be sacrificed to rats.'

Furlough was intended to be a time of respite from the daily privations of life in Angola, a chance to rest and recuperate and recharge her batteries. In her first eleven years of service, she only managed to get home twice, once for nine months and once for a month. It hadn't been enough, and as the cycle of war, supposed peace and war again, continued, she was advised to try to find time for more regular breaks. They helped her to step back and look more objectively at the situation in Angola, when she wasn't in the middle of running rings around herself. It was a time for reflection and prayer in order to return renewed and reinvigorated. She was always grateful for those that 'showered her with love and support and those who gave her a listening ear.' She always spent some time at the start catching up on her backlog of emails and letters: thanking people for gifts she'd received, telling them what she'd done (or was doing) with the money, passing on the most recent news of the work and providing specific points for prayer. There were also family needs which she tried to meet in the short months of being home, aware that when she was away the burden fell on other family members. As the only daughter, her mum and her gran were obviously important to her, and on one furlough she was able to help them move into more suitable accommodation. She was glad of that on her own account too, for the new house was warm, which made the transition from a hot Angola to a cold Cornwall easier. Initially she enjoyed walking out the front door without being met by a crowd of folk clamouring for help of various kinds. But it usually wasn't long before she was missing them!

In 2017 it was rather different. She was fairly well up to date with acknowledgements, and aside from giving a short update on what had happened in the six weeks she'd been back in Angola, her main news and prayer requests focused on her health situation. She sat on the settee in her lounge, in the peace and quiet, her laptop on her knee. Various papers and letters were spread out on the seat beside her, not competing for space with school books to be marked, notes of things which needed to be done, and sundry electrical or plumbing bits and pieces, or car parts, which had been strewn on every available surface in her house in Saurimo. As she worked her way through the emails, without any interruption in power supply, she thought of how important, yet often very difficult, communications had been in Angola.

Angola: Communications

Mail had always been a problem, the postal service from outside the country so slow that when she'd first arrived letters took up to two months to reach Biula, and packages often didn't arrive at all. A solution (of a sort) had been found. Parcels were sent to missionaries in Zambia in a sealed container, marked as 'In transit to Angola'. Someone from Zambia then drove to the Angolan border to pass them on. It was no quicker, but it was cheaper and also helped to ensure nothing was siphoned off en route. Once they'd made the move to Luanda due to the escalation of hostilities, letters also became an issue.

In a communist state there was always the risk that opinions which appeared at odds with government policy would invite censure at best and reprisals at worst. It was especially important to Ruth, as a single person, to be able to communicate with folk at home and to share specific prayer requests. Sometimes, however, they referred to sensitive matters, and when it was clear that her letters were being opened and resealed before leaving the country, she knew she needed to look for alternative ways to get news out that wouldn't pose a risk to herself or others. She took the opportunity when anyone was going out of the country to send letters with them to be posted outside Angola. That meant that news to home was often less frequent than either she or they would have liked.

Communications, both within and outside the country, continued to be a problem throughout the war years, even when the risk of interception had diminished. There was no effective postal service at Saurimo, so once again mail could only be sent or received if either Ruth or Mary went down to Luanda to send it out from there and to pick up mail that had arrived from the UK. There were lengthy periods when news from Ruth was sporadic at best. She wasn't terribly good at writing letters regularly anyway. When she was tired, as she often was, letter writing tended to be pushed to the bottom of her 'to-do' list. A high proportion of her letters, when they did arrive, began with an apology for the length of time since she last wrote. It was clear that she kept so many balls in the air it was very difficult for her to have the time (or the energy) for correspondence at the end of a long day's work. The fact that delivery was uncertain was an added disincentive to write them at all.

However, she loved receiving letters, and was very disappointed when she found that a box containing food and letters, which had been left for her in a container in Luanda, had been eaten by rats. She was '*sure the rats had been the better for it*', but commented '*letters are too precious a commodity to be sacrificed to rats.*'

By May 1994 she had a radio, which was extremely useful. However, she felt as much constrained in terms of what she could say over the airwaves as she had been in letters. Freedom of speech is something we take for granted, or at least we did until recently with the rise of 'woke' and 'cancel culture', but for missionaries on the ground in a country with a communist heritage, what they could or should and shouldn't say was a serious consideration. Several years later, with the war still in full swing, a trust in the UK offered to send out a satellite phone, which potentially would solve the problems of communication, though not the issue of content.

The promise and delivery of a satellite phone was a 'high point', but the repeated failure to get it to work in conjunction with her computer as a fax machine, and the eventual confirmation that the phone she'd been given wasn't compatible with her computer, was a 'low'. There was an option of an 'all-singing, all-dancing' system which included phone, fax and email and which would, undoubtedly, make communication much more straightfor-ward. It was, however, the most expensive option, and it required the buying of prepaid minutes on top of a service charge every month. There were two other fax machines that would work with her existing phone, one of which didn't require any paper rolls – a definite bonus in a remote area of Angola. It was a difficult decision, for Ruth felt somewhat guilty at money being used for her own needs and on something she couldn't help feeling was a 'luxury' when she was surrounded by people with so many basic needs. In the end, the argument in favour of purchasing a system was won by the absence of local medical backup, and the ability it would provide to get immediate telephone advice in the event of an emergency.

It was 1997 when a compatible satellite phone / fax system was delivered, but setting it up wasn't straightforward. There were pages of technical instructions, some of which needed to be done in the UK before it was shipped, others which applied on site. They varied from what seemed relatively easy – the length and specific cable required – to the more intimidating – the requirement for silver-plated, military-specification connectors. Where and how the antenna should be sited, the compatibility or otherwise with various versions of Windows, the satellite requirements, and a host of other technical 'gobbledegook' was as good as Greek to Ruth. The warning in capitals not to have it sent to Angola until it had all been commissioned and thoroughly tested in the UK, preferably by a professional, left her thinking it would be a miracle if it could be set up at all. By the time it was installed they found it needed a compulsory upgrade – as there was a new satellite – so she was asked could she get the unit to Zambia as someone was going there to upgrade systems and could do hers at the same time. This story was one that ran and ran…

Eventually it was operational and was, in Ruth's words, *'brilliant when it worked.'* Clearly there were times when it didn't, cutting her off from the missionaries in Luanda and from home. Unfortunately, the cost of using it was high, as she had to pay both for sending and receiving emails. Fine if they were emails she intended to send or wanted to receive. Not so good when she had to pay anything between £5–£20 for incoming 'junk' mail. In one month, the satellite phone bill was an eye-watering £800. As a result, Ruth preferred to have two emails – one general, that she only picked up when she was in Luanda and could access via a landline, and a second one only given to family and those who needed to be able to keep in touch with her at all times.

Chapter Seven

'Usoko Waha'
'A New Family'

Angola: Family matters

Ruth knew from the start that serving God as a missionary would mean leaving her 'home and brothers and sisters and mother and father'[3] and she was prepared for that. It didn't make it any easier for her to be far away, however, especially at the times when family members were seriously ill. In 1996 both her father and her sister-in-law were unwell. She would have liked to be able to support them, but she made the very difficult decision to hold off her visit home until later in the year, in order to help with the building work in Angola, for when there was no one to supervise, mistakes were made or shortcuts taken.

The importance of family funerals has been brought into sharp focus in the UK by the 2020 Covid-19 pandemic, with the restrictions on gatherings, even for funerals, and the very public anguish many people suffered.

When Ruth's father died, she was on her own, with Mary and Brian and Debbie all on furlough, so she was grateful for a couple from her home church who 'held the fort' in Angola, enabling her to go home for a flying visit to be

---

3   Matthew ch 19 v 29

with her family. She was also able to fly home for her mother's funeral, but what touched Ruth most at that time was the outpouring of love for her by the Angolans. Many elders came bringing gifts of money from their churches – a cultural expression of sympathy – while others brought food gifts for the mourning process. Some men came nearly two hundred kilometres to bring her manioc meal, a chicken and a goat. Although grateful, she didn't know where to keep them overnight, afraid her guard dogs would tear them to pieces. She was relieved to find them still alive the next morning and had fun getting them into the car to take them to Camundambala, where they could be of more use. As Chokwes rarely said thank you for anything, these expressions of love and sympathy were heart-warming and left her feeling it was a privilege to serve them.

Cornwall, 2017

One of Ruth's passions had always been watching football, so when she came home for assessment and treatment, while she was still able, she watched as many matches as she could. The team she supported was West Ham, but she was happy to watch any Premier League games, and was somewhat disgruntled to find that, now with some time for leisure on her hands, many matches were no longer shown live on UK terrestrial TV. She wasn't a passive viewer. Instead, she would get thoroughly involved and, as she might have done had she been at a match in person, would react vocally to every near miss, or poor pass, and shout advice at the players, the coaches, and the referees.

For many years in Angola she didn't have any access to televised sport, but when she eventually got a TV and was (sort of) able to access satellite broadcasts, she would sometimes watch a football match with Brian Howden and his two boys. His wife Debbie wasn't interested in football, but she was needed to stand, for the entire duration of the match, holding the aerial above her head wherever the best signal was, boosting it by being an aerial herself! Many of Ruth's letters to those who shared her interest, particularly in the post-war period, closed off with a comment on football, especially commiserations or congratulations as appropriate for their favourite team. Although Ruth was totally dedicated to the people of Angola and the work she did there, this glimpse into an interest of hers, even though she had little time to indulge in it, provides a very human touch.

Just as her love of football had been a bridge to enable her to get alongside some of the younger lads when she first arrived at Biula, so her interest in sport generally and her heart for young people led her to set up her backyard as a space for teenagers, with a pool table and a table tennis table. She recognised that providing a safe environment for teenagers to 'hang out', in itself an important social function, was also a means of encouraging them spiritually. In the Chokwe culture, parents don't generally play with their children, even when they are quite young, so to be given space to enjoy themselves was both novel and important for the lads who came to her yard. Many of the teenage boys from the various churches in Saurimo spent a lot of their free time there, and as a result started doing Bible studies, first using Emmaus courses then moving on to Ruth's discipleship and leadership training classes. There were about a dozen lads in particular who over time she trusted to have the run of her yard whether she was at home or not. They eventually formed the core of the group whom, once peace was established, she took out to villages to run Sunday schools. She encouraged them in other ways too – seeing the potential of each one and suggesting appropriate jobs or further study for them. Some she encouraged to go to college, some to become teachers, others she taught to drive and ultimately employed. When I interviewed a number of these lads to ask them about Ruth and what she meant to them and had done for them, they all said very similar things: 'She was our mother'; 'She loved us and lived among us'; 'We owe all our Bible knowledge to her'; 'She gave us responsibility'; and most important of all: 'Everything I know about living a Christian life came from her teaching and her example.' They are an important part of Ruth's legacy to the churches in Chokweland, but just as she was important to them, they were also important to her. In a very real sense, they became the children that she never had, and she was justly proud of the young men they became.

The missionary 'family' in Angola was never large, and one of the most difficult things for Ruth was to say goodbye to missionaries relocating or retiring. She had always known that the missionaries already at Biula when she arrived would retire long before her service was finished, and she wasn't surprised when the war brought George and Ena's retirement forward. But it was a particularly difficult wrench to lose Becky when she retired to Canada after being in Angola for fifty years. It was extremely hard for Becky too. Ruth went down to Luanda to help her pack up, and she found it difficult watching Becky as she went through the emotional breaking up of a large chunk of her life, knowing there was no one to carry on some of her projects. There were lighter moments too, when they went through some boxes and found food that was well beyond its 'best before' date but still edible. Ruth noted that Becky 'worked her way through the Bran Flakes, while I suffered the chocolate'. Becky had been much loved by Angolans and missionaries alike. At her last day in the church fellowship she attended, many Angolans wept throughout the service. She had also been an essential lynchpin in Luanda, dealing with all the goods that came through the port, as well as any visitors and liaising with the Angolan church leaders. Her retirement not only left a huge gap, but it meant Ruth became the 'senior' missionary. Responsibility for all the mission work associated with the Brethren Church of Angola fell to her, including what to do about the Angolans who had worked with Becky. She couldn't afford to keep them all on, nor supervise them from Saurimo, but it was difficult to tell some they no longer had a job. There was also the issue of Becky's house and, trivial as it may seem, what to do about her dog!

Ruth was very aware of the tension between her own desire for more workers and the understanding of how difficult things were in the country. With the need so great, it would have been easy to welcome any potential new workers with open arms. However, there were many complex considerations that parents in particular had to take into account when weighing up if their 'call' was from God. Ruth knew from her own experience that to survive and be truly useful to God in Angola required a clear call, not simply an emotional response to the undoubted need. Several times when Ruth was home on furlough, she met up with couples who were considering going out to Angola and, though she battled with mixed emotions, took the difficult decision to suggest they shouldn't do it. In one case she made the decision on health grounds. In another, she felt she must be honest as to the issues their teenage children would face. She summarised the difficulties as grappling with a different culture, language, mentality and church settings. In both those cases the prospective missionaries took her advice and went on to serve God elsewhere.

When Ruth had first met Brian and Debbie Howden, in the early 1990s, she had misgivings, fearing that Debbie – who was petite and elegant, in contrast to Ruth, who was physically robust and strong – wouldn't be able to cope with the living conditions. Despite her human concerns, she hadn't felt any inner sense that she should voice them and had been delighted when she'd been proved wrong. Their 'call' was real, and their willingness to answer it and bring a young family into the difficult and potentially dangerous situation had been both an encouragement and a joy. Over the next eight years she'd appreciated their company and loved having their children to entertain and be an 'auntie' to. As boys, she could relate to them easily, drawing on her own childhood experiences with her brothers. She missed them when they took their boys home for secondary schooling in 2003 but recognised it was the right thing to do.

In 2016, after thirteen years of Brian coming back and forwards for a few months at a time, he and Debbie returned to full-time service in Camundambala, and both they and Ruth looked forward to working together until Ruth would retire. They returned at a time when Angola once again faced financial problems, due in part to mismanagement and corruption, but also by being seriously impacted by falling oil prices – which was the main source of government income. Financial controls made it illegal to take foreign currency out of the country, and many shops closed down as they couldn't import new stock. Once again there were shortages and rampant inflation, the cost of even the basics rocketing. A sack of rice which previously had cost 3,500 kwanzas had shot up to 11,000 kwanzas. All foreigners who had dollar accounts had to withdraw money from the banks in kwanzas. The official government exchange rate was 500 kwanzas to the dollar but the bank only gave 160 kwanzas to the dollar – so bank transfers were no longer of much use. As a result, anyone visiting was asked to bring in dollars, up to the legal limit. In the country as a whole, salaries had fallen to one quarter of previous levels, in buying terms, and many Angolans were once again in dire straits, although the elite rich were as rich as ever. It was dispiriting that fourteen years after the end of the war the living conditions for ordinary people hadn't improved. The feeding programme for lepers and the elderly at Camundambala, which Ruth had taken responsibility for, remained a vital lifeline. The difficult conditions had spawned a big rise in burglaries, including at the Emmaus office and print room. It was broken into several times, and after the number of doors was increased and burglar bars installed, the would-be thieves came through the roof! As they only found Bibles and books, nothing was taken.

It was into this climate of continued uncertainty that two new families arrived to join the missionary team. One family was relocating from Zambia and one coming to Africa for the first time. Initially they settled at Biula. It was a long-awaited answer to prayer but hadn't proved straightforward. The family from Zambia was initially refused a letter of invitation by the Angolan church administration, and though that was resolved, Ruth was concerned how they would be received by the local church. She wondered if, coming from a background of fully autonomous church fellowships, they would cope with the need for formal recognition by the government. There were also the difficulties posed by the Angolan culture and more primitive living conditions than those they had experienced during their years in Zambia, where there had been undisturbed peace for a century, with established missions and comfortable houses. They had a large family, with teenage boys and a primary age daughter, so the accommodation currently available posed a challenge. The Chokwes were also much more demanding in character than the Zambians, and lacked their politeness. Ruth knew it would be a steep learning curve for them, and as the 'senior' missionary she did her best to ease the transition, both for them and their children and for the other family that had come to Africa for the first time.

Both couples and Ruth, as the receiving missionary, faced additional pressures from the Angolan church hierarchy, who felt they should be able to dictate where the new couples were based. And as the wives were nurses, they expected them to work in the medical clinic. They, however, felt they should prioritise the home schooling of their children. Ruth supported them in this. It was understandable from a Western perspective but was less clear from an Angolan one. Working through tensions of this nature, that arise from differing cultural expectations, was (and still is) an unavoidable part of the missionary experience, requiring cultural sensitivity, tact and the willingness to compromise.

Ruth intended to retire in 2026, when she would reach seventy, and had discussed her 'succession' planning with the trustees of the charity that channelled funds to her. Her aim remained, as it had always been, to hand over as much as possible of her work to local Angolans. Several stages had been completed: control of the Emmaus work was in the hands of locals, though still externally funded, and some 400 men had already passed through her training course for church leaders, using a six-book series called A Workman Approved, which came from Brazil.

Most of the teachers in the schools were now on government salaries, and the clinics were now the responsibility of the government, but there was still a lot of work for mission personnel. The school building at Camundambala was well past its 'best before' date. There wasn't any realistic possibility of either local funding or expertise to replace it. Ruth, though not knowing her time of service was coming to an end, nevertheless felt it was too big a job for her to take on for a second time. Instead, she sketched out a plan of what she felt was needed and passed the responsibility for implementing it to Brian. She hoped to continue encouraging and providing guidance for the teachers at the school, as well as supporting literacy work, particularly among women, and the feeding programme at the leper village.

It's impossible to write about the work in Angola without a general reference to finances. Looking back, Ruth was staggered at the amount of money she handled, but the needs were so great that she felt blessed by the provision. In other countries the money coming through would have been spread among a number of people, but in Angola, for much of her time, all the money from the UK was channelled through her. It was a huge responsibility, not least in determining how to divide up the available funds, but one which she sought to fulfil in a way that would honour God.

Chapter Eight

'Kumeso lia lamba linji'
'In the face of such suffering'

It's interesting to see how much of Ruth's work and how many of her letters were focused on practical issues. It was an out-working of the verse – 'Whatever you do, work at it with all your heart as working for the Lord.'[4] Our Western culture often makes false distinctions between 'spiritual' and 'non-spiritual' tasks and assigns a higher value to the former, but it isn't only by preaching that the gospel can be communicated. Ruth learnt through the years of war and the terrible suffering of those around her that following Jesus also involved following His example of compassion and care for the whole person – physical, emotional and spiritual. This was clearly illustrated by the amount of time, effort and money Ruth devoted to humanitarian needs.

Cornwall, 2017

Ruth had been home for six weeks. She'd had the results of the scans, which at that stage were fairly positive as her major organs remained clear, and was preparing to begin her treatment. She and one of her brothers had their birthdays in the same week, so it was the ideal opportunity to have a meal out with her family. Ruth had always enjoyed her food and was particularly keen on a roast dinner. Visitors that she'd cooked roasts for in Angola, when it was

---

4   Colossians ch 3 v 23

possible to obtain any meat, reported that her Yorkshire puddings were 'to die for'. As she queued at the carvery in the Rashleigh at Charlestown, and saw the array of meats and vegetables on offer, she couldn't help but remember the war years in Angola, when getting any food at all had been difficult, and the idea of choice unimaginable.

Angola: Humanitarian needs

At Biula, with UNITA close by, the team at the mission station had become almost totally dependent on food parcels sent out from the UK. Often, they didn't get through, but when they did, it was an opportunity to help some of the villagers. In June 1984 Ruth wrote, '*Three food parcels arrived. We cooked four packets of dried meat, to feed those most in need.*' It's hard to imagine how critical the shortages were, and what a difference even one containerload from the UK made. Or how hard it must have been to have to choose who to feed.

Sometimes it was the little things that were disproportionally distressing, like the young man who visited Ruth in 1990 wearing a pair of second-hand ladies' white sandals because it was all he could find in his size. It had been six years since it was possible to buy a pair of shoes anywhere in Lunda Sul province, and household items such as soap and pots and pans were also in short supply. Some of those who had fled because of attacks on their villages had only what they stood up in, and even their clothing was often in tatters. Many were without even a blanket to cover them at night. When Mary returned from Luanda in May 1990 on a military flight, complete with the contents of a container, they were able to send out the second-hand pots and pans, clothes and blankets to some of the worst-hit areas. And although it only scratched the surface of the needs, it was an encouragement to the churches, a sign that neither God, nor their fellow Christians in the West, had forgotten them. They were excited by the parcels of packet soup, dried meat and rice that were in the container, and the biggest thrill of all was the 'Instant Whip' that could be made up with dried milk powder. Throughout Ruth's time in Angola, she divided the gifts she got into three – for literature, especially Bibles; for the 'needy'; and for her personal needs; but often she used the personal gifts for either of the other two, seeing them as more important.

By 1990 most things could be bought in Luanda, at a price, but in the interior it was very different. In an attempt to buy up supplies of food and essentials Ruth flew down to Luanda on a Mission Aviation Fellowship flight. At nearly £1,000 per flight, it wasn't something she could do regularly, but it was the only viable option at the time. She had intended her trip to be brief, and she used money sent out from the UK to buy sacks of rice and beans and baby milk. The latter was for babies orphaned through the mother's death in childbirth, or whose mothers had no milk due to illnesses such as TB. But the MAF return flight failed as they hadn't been able to get the giant oxygen bottles required to allow them to fly, and five weeks later she was still trying to find a way to get back to Saurimo. She pinned her hopes on the Catholic Church, which was chartering a plane to get their supplies through and had offered her a place on it, as well as space for one ton of cargo. But as the days slid into weeks, she became increasingly frustrated and thought maybe she should just forget the cargo and go back and live on whatever they could find locally. Knowing their health and strength depended on a reasonable diet, and that the supplies were vital for so many others also, common sense prevailed, and she continued to trail out to the airport each day in the hope a plane would actually fly.

By the time MAF were finally able to fly, she had used more funds for the 'needy' to buy tins of sardines and to pay for the freight of 120 kilos of dried fish, 50 kilos of salt, and dried milk bought in the markets in Luanda. For the people in Saurimo the supplies couldn't have come at a better time, for the government had just devalued the currency and the shops were empty. Local markets weren't functioning either, as no one wanted to sell anything they'd managed to produce until they knew the value of the new money. In order to help hungry people in town, Ruth and Mary went out to a village with some clothes to barter for manioc, which villagers started to fight over. Twice to keep some order she put everything away and threatened to leave. It was extremely upsetting to see that the clothes were so needed that the people would have given any amount of manioc for them. Shortages and exorbitant prices were the norm. A tin of cooking oil which cost 3,000 kwanzas before the war had shot up to 35,000 kwanzas, and two manioc roots were selling for 10,000 kwanzas. Ruth and Mary sourced food locally when they could, despite the exorbitant prices, for that in itself was a help to those around them. But much of the food and clothing aid came in the containers that Medical Missionary News shipped from the UK.

Aid was given irrespective of any religious belief or none, and it was essential to work closely with others in order not to duplicate it. Transport remained a huge problem and limited what they could do. The UN no longer flew inland, though the Lutheran World Federation still brought a plane once a month and gave Ruth and Mary two sacks of milk and two boxes of protein biscuits each time. They would also carry aid sent from the UK for them when they had space. To offload it, the truck was driven onto the tarmac and stopped under the hold of the plane. Several workers stood on the truck and the sacks or drums of aid were slid down their backs to others waiting below. Ruth and Mary also tried to move supplies on government planes, but the cost was generally prohibitive and the risks high, for stealing was rife, gunfire prolific and general lawlessness a serious, hampering issue.

Such was the black-market price of food and medicines, troops, who were often young conscripts, hung about the airport waiting for the opportunity to steal humanitarian aid to use or to sell. In classic understatement, Ruth wrote of the difficulties of loading and offloading, 'Grappling with armed men isn't fun', but she didn't hesitate to do it when the need arose. A colleague recounted one occasion when, having filled the truck from the plane, Ruth was about to drive off when she saw a soldier scrambling onto the back and grabbing a sack. She immediately stopped the truck, leapt out and, catching hold of him, pulled him back and retrieved the sack.

There were times when Ruth was tempted to wonder if humanitarian aid was what they should be focusing on, for it seemed far from the spiritual work she had come to Angola to do. She had to keep reminding herself that if she didn't continue she would be cutting huge tracts of Jesus's teaching out of the Bible. The humanitarian aid was a practical out-working of giving 'a cup of water in My name'.[5] The numbers of refugees continued to increase and Ruth was thankful for a gift from the UK which enabled them to provide a hundred of them with one meal per day for two weeks. A drop in the ocean of need, but a blessing nonetheless.

By 1994, travel, even for short distances into the countryside, had become impossible again. Thankfully, as the flood of refugees into the town and surrounding camps continued, the UN recommended flying and brought in one planeload of supplies per day.

---

5   Mark ch 9 v 41

The problems in Saurimo, however, were dwarfed by those in the tiny town of Cafunfo, which had been under government control for nine months, completely encircled by UNITA forces. In all that time they had no access to food or medicines. Ruth was alerted to the situation when one of the missionaries in Luanda received a letter from a Christian in the town. They immediately passed the word to UNAVEM and through them to other NGOs. An NGO team went in to verify the report and brought out heart-rending photographs of emaciation, which indicated severe malnutrition. Some immediate aid was arranged, and as there were quite a number of independent churches in the area, Ruth and her fellow missionaries were asked if they could go to coordinate the distribution. Ruth initially volunteered to go for a week, but the Lutheran World Federation asked her to stay for a month until their coordinator arrived. A gift of £1,000 which had just arrived from the UK intended for Saurimo was used to buy three tons of rice, beans, salt and soap for Cafunfo instead. It enabled the feeding programme to begin immediately, as it would be another ten days before the LWF aid would arrive.

Ruth and Tito, an Angolan worker, were flown in by the UN in a small Cessna and circled high above the town while the pilot made radio contact with UN forces on the ground. He was warned of a river he mustn't cross while coming in to land, and once he had pinpointed it, they came down in tighter and tighter spirals, the engines screaming. Cafunfo had two runways; the first was originally tarmac, but now it was no more than a series of craters, with wrecked military vehicles strewn across it. They were cleared to land on the second, soil runway, which had been swept for mines for their approach. They touched down with relief, but also a sense of foreboding as to what they would find in the town.

It was a diamond mine town, once rigidly controlled by the government, the population restricted to 5,000. But since 1990, following the collapse of communism, private diamond mining had been legal, and a diamond 'rush' meant that by 1992 the population had swelled to 40,000. There were two independent churches, and every surrounding village also had either a church or a preaching point served by a number of dedicated local brethren. When Ruth had visited with George and Ena and Eric and Margaret in 1992, there had been 1,000 Christians gathered together to worship in one of the town churches. But, due to the collapse of the peace following the disputed election, and the resultant fighting in the surrounding area, the town had shrunk again to around 8,000, with a further 4,000 people in accessible surrounding villages. A nutritional survey showed that 50 per cent of the population were suffering from either malnutrition or severe malnutrition. The particular tragedy of Cafunfo was that the population had money, because of the diamond mining, and could have afforded to buy food, but children and weaker adults were dying of hunger because they couldn't access it.

The government troops, though fed by parachute drop, had also taken any food that could be found close by. Permission was granted from both sides to allow food aid in to save the starving population, but flying was still very hazardous. Two Hercules planes came per week, but before each flight the soil runway had to be swept for mines. Each Hercules could bring eighteen tons of food, but the men in the town were initially too weak to lift much. At the beginning it took four men to lift a fifty-kilogramme sack (the weight of a sack of coal) and fifteen to get a 200-litre drum of fuel onto the back of a Toyota. If the larger truck wasn't available it took eighteen trips to transport the aid from the airport to the warehouse, so on days without the truck it was a major headache to keep the kitchens supplied with sacks of milk, biscuits, porridge, firewood and water. There were four workers in all – Ruth and Tito and two workers from the Lutheran World Federation – and for a month they barely stopped for breath.

When they'd first arrived the death toll in the two churches alone was standing at seven people per day, but as they were fed it gradually decreased, and Ruth was moved by the joy and relief on people's faces.

The LWF set up two food kitchens – one in each of the churches in town – to distribute milk, nutritional biscuits and specially constituted 'porridge'. Each kitchen served a thousand people. Additional dry rations were also supplied and the Christians among them poured out their hearts in gratitude to God for sending people to help them in their time of need.

After a month there was a dramatic difference in the population; their swollen legs and white hair returning to normal, and their physical strength and stamina increasing. For Ruth it was yet another reason to pray for peace, that the people of Angola might be released from the terrible suffering and pressure they were under. She knew that until their physical needs were catered for many would not be able to hold fast to faith. And yet she saw some who were steadfast, despite the circumstances, and thanked God for them. One village elder oversaw one of the kitchens. His wife, three children, two nieces and his sister had all been killed when the government bombed his village. Ruth was at a loss to know what to say to him in the face of such an enormous tragedy. It was a humbling experience when on the Sunday morning he got up in church, the building pockmarked by bullet holes and with only half a roof, and poured out his heart to God in worship, praise and thanksgiving for His love. It was both a privilege and a challenge to work alongside men like him.

Each Sunday they visited a different church. Not one building had an intact roof, the walls peppered with shrapnel holes, and yet the people still gathered to worship. It was an evidence of faith that Christians in the West could learn a lot from.

At the end of the month Iris Floyd arrived to take over the responsibility for the gradual reduction in the kitchens, though the dry rations distribution would continue. Ruth was released to return to Saurimo and was encouraged to find that the Christians there had been having special prayer times to pray for safety in Cafunfo because of the security issues.

In Saurimo, the World Food Programme continued to provide food for the most vulnerable, and all the churches in the town got an allocation, but this needed to be coordinated and supervised. A modern Western approach would look to locals to organise the food distribution, and perhaps criticise the WFP, who required an expatriate to supervise. But with so much hunger, it was hard to get Angolans, even church leaders, who could be trusted to do the job honestly. There was an inappropriate, but understandable, temptation to supply their family and friends with more than their share of the allocation. Ruth, while sympathising with the need, had a running battle with one church which produced a list of 188 people over seventy (the criteria for WFP aid). The actual church membership of all ages was only about fifty. The elders had made a fake list so they could receive the food and resell it to buy other necessities. It took almost two months to sort that church out and was a strain on both Ruth's time and her emotional resources. But it was essential to step in to these situations, otherwise the really needy wouldn't have got the aid they required.

Following on from the work they did at Cafunfo, UNICEF requested help to distribute aid in the Cacolo area, but Ruth decided it was important to visit first, to see how they could work through the churches, before she would commit to anything. A bi-annual conference, with elders from all over

Angola, had illustrated how widespread the suffering was as a result of the bitter fighting, and it was humbling to hear how the Christians in the various areas had responded to such suffering.

It was left to Ruth to determine how money sent from the UK and designated as 'for the needy' should be allocated. It was a difficult task, for most of the population she lived among were, in Western terms, 'needy'. When peace finally came, Christians who had been forced into refugee camps by the government were cut off from any food from the WFP and told to return home. They weren't offered any free transport and the cost in the case of one group to return to their original area was £15 per person. It doesn't sound much to us, but it was entirely out of their reach. Their alternative was a walk of 120 kilometres, so Ruth covered their transport costs. She was conscious that longer-term solutions were equally as important as fulfilling immediate need. So, as well as helping people to return to their villages, she wanted to help them to rebuild homes and churches destroyed by the war. And to provide them with a means of earning a living, she bought tools for carpentry, building and mechanics.

In a country without social care, the elderly and the sick were particularly vulnerable. By 2004 she was running a feeding programme for a number of old women, some who had been abandoned by their families due to accusations of witchcraft, and some who had previously received food aid along with their TB treatment but were no longer receiving it. Each month she bought them supplies of cornmeal, rice, oil, beans, salt, sugar and tins of sardines. Lepers were also vulnerable, and in 2006 Ruth took over responsibility for the leper village at Camundambala. It required a significant financial outlay, and although she was initially apprehensive, she was able, with help from Brian and Debbie and a leprosy mission, to provide food for them also.

When she surveyed the houses in the leper village, she found most in poor condition and lacking basic furniture and household goods. The renovations of the houses varied according to condition, including re-roofing, new cement floors, replacement windows and doors, repainting, and the shoring up of foundations, exposed by heavy rains. The plan was also to build an external kitchen for each house, where cooking could be done on charcoal, as well as build a pit latrine. It was a rolling programme of decanting and rehousing the lepers as the houses were fixed. Those who had moved back in were delighted, and called that section of the village the 'city', as the houses looked so good. The household items she bought were very basic – buckets, bowls, cups, plates, cutlery and pans, as well as beds or mattresses, but those who received them were thrilled. Ruth continued to organise the feeding and building work at the leper village, including the renovation of the water system. But as it took up quite a bit of her time, she employed a man to oversee the food distribution on her behalf. Unfortunately, what should have relieved the pressure on her increased it. The man in charge disappeared for six weeks without telling anyone and took the keys to the storehouse with him, leaving them with no access to either the food or the building materials. Eventually, after four weeks, Ruth had to break into the store, and when he came back, she paid and sacked him simultaneously; for an unreliable worker was worse than no worker at all.

Brian and Debbie continue the feeding programme and the renovation of spare houses at the leper village to provide accommodation for others in need, including an elderly widow who had been a faithful worker at Biula and for young Christians wishing to marry and have a house of their own.

Chapter Nine

'Ndako ni ufulielo'
'Superstition, tradition and faith'

Cornwall, 2017

Ruth had been home for a couple of months before the effects of the chemother-apy stopped her from being able to go out other than for hospital visits. She had enjoyed attending her home church, able, for a change, just to sit and listen to the various preachers, their knowledge of and familiarity with the Bible clear. She wondered how many of the congregation knew just how fortunate they were.

Angola: The Chokwe church

Ruth knew there were problems in many Chokwe churches, but it wasn't until she was living at Saurimo that the true extent became clear. Writing home, she summarised the state of the country in four sentences:

> *Angola, potentially rich, with a population of over 12 million, torn by civil wars since 1961, is a country of vast needs, where extreme wealth sits side by side with extreme poverty. Diamond and oil revenues supply smart cars, satellite dishes, big houses and trips abroad to some. The majority, however, struggle to survive another day – with little healthcare, education or resources of any sort. Needs of every kind hit you in the face day after day – and not least*

among these deeply felt needs is the great lack and therefore great
difficulty in obtaining Christian literature, be it Bibles or books.

She wrote of the struggles of Angolan Christians in the wake of war, persecution, isolation and a dearth of Bible teachers, and how vulnerable it had made them to the infiltration of pagan and traditional beliefs into the churches. There was evidence of the legacy of the various missions over the years, and some well-grounded Christians, but the majority of professing Christians, including many church elders, especially in rural areas cut off for so many years by war, were ignorant of basic Bible truths. They had 'believed' but weren't sure in what. There were wrong doctrines and wrong practices, and all sorts of strange customs had crept into the services, as well as personal issues such as witchcraft, drunkenness and corruption, even among some church elders. A few men who tried to take control of all the churches in the area, and to insist on the right to carry out all marriages and baptisms, were an additional problem. Their motives were financial, as they charged a chicken or a goat for the privilege.

Some concepts, good in principle, had become corrupted. Young children were sent to pre-baptismal 'Yihula' (Question) classes. In a society with high levels of illiteracy, it was the only way for children to learn the basics of the Christian faith. But the 'questions' provided a very limited knowledge of the gospel, particularly in the case of the child of a church elder who was only expected to attend classes for six weeks instead of the more normal one or two years. They were then presented for baptism, irrespective of any expression of personal faith. Specific rituals and superstitions surrounded the baptismal service itself. At the riverside the water was 'blessed'; there was a prayer asking the Holy Spirit to be upon the one carrying out the baptism; and the child was told that they were passing from death to life. Though there were parallels with practices in some mainstream Christian denominations, it didn't reflect the New Testament principle that the brethren churches followed that baptism should follow a confession of faith.

There were other, harder to explain superstitions – when a child came up out of the water they had to keep their hands together and not wipe the water from their eyes or else they would have what was termed a 'bad' baptism. If they stumbled in the water, or looked back towards the river, they would soon lose their faith. Once out of the water they were led into the long grass to change into new clothes and bury their old ones. In the few months since coming to Saurimo, Mary and Ruth had attended three baptismal services and knew of two more, with a total of more than 500 children of varying ages baptised. It would have been easy for her to criticise the form of what was happening rather than tackling the underlying philosophy. But she felt strongly that it was an example of the paganising of the Church.

One of the main problems was that the Christian concepts of death to sin and resurrection to a new life in Christ had become tangled up with the traditional Bantu rites of passage from child to adult, linked to circumcision camps. Boys reaching puberty were separated from their community and taken off into the bush and remained there for up to two months. At the start they were circumcised by 'priests' chosen by the village chief, and while they healed physically, they acted as if they knew nothing of their previous life in order to identify with death. They were instructed in all the wisdom of the elders and their responsibilities within the community as husband, father, farmer, hunter. They learnt about myths and genealogies and tribal taboos and magic and were sexually initiated, seen as a spiritual act sacred to the ancestors.

This symbolic 'death' was followed by rites of resurrection and new life and a reintroduction into the 'clan'. Those who passed through these rites took a new name and were sworn to secrecy regarding the rites they had passed through. They burned their temporary camp and their mothers welcomed them back with new clothes, feasting and dancing, a sign that the new birth was complete. It wasn't hard to find parallels, though the linking of new birth to sexual acts was particularly shocking.

The Biblical story of Nicodemus coming to Jesus by night was misapplied to show that spiritual rebirth was also for those who came together by night, with the result that nocturnal orgies were held, and even incest was permitted in the name of the new birth experience. It was difficult for Ruth to combat this, for it was culturally inappropriate for a woman to speak to men of such things.

Another, less insidious, but nevertheless concerning superstition became clear when Ruth was asked for the exact date of the death of an early missionary. It seemed that many believed miracles would happen at his grave on the anniversary of his death. Even government officials had gone hoping for cures. Countering this erroneous mix of superstition, traditional rites and Christian faith was an ongoing battle.

In her lowest moments, struggling to know how to tackle these issues, she questioned why no one was coming to help, and she concluded that God was calling but Christians weren't answering. On a human level she understood the lack of appeal of a country torn apart by war. Safety couldn't be guaranteed and food and basic necessities were often unobtainable. The housing was basic, at best, and spiritual problems, including the rising tide of witchcraft, were multiplying. None of which made the isolation and feelings of inadequacy any easier to bear. But the answer, as always, was to refocus on her own call, and on God's promise – 'My Grace is sufficient for you, for My power is made perfect in weakness.'[6]

Time after time, when she reached 'rock bottom' in terms of her own resources, God stepped in with encouragement to keep her going. In 1990, disregarding the potential danger, three young men, who had no means of transport, walked some forty kilometres from Saurimo to a village to preach. The villagers were so afraid of mines or of being captured by UNITA that they didn't travel outside their village and so were completely isolated. They were thrilled to receive a visit and made a meal of funge (the Angolan staple made of manioc) for the visitors three times that night. The young men had arrived on the Saturday and preached all afternoon and around the campfires in the evening. Moved by their welcome, they stayed up all night, singing, answering questions and teaching the Scriptures. After sharing in the Sunday services they walked home again, exhilarated by the experience.

In 1991, Eric and Margaret came up to Saurimo to spend some time with Ruth and Mary. Their fellowship and Eric's Bible teaching were high points. They all managed to visit both Luena and Biula, to find the Christians there were remaining faithful to the word of God, and despite the suffering of the war they enjoyed their worship services and focused simply on Christ, without the 'add-ons' Ruth struggled against at Saurimo. It inspired Ruth to keep going despite the difficulties, and despite her longing for Eric or another man to be able to stay in Saurimo full-time to be available to advise Angolan men on issues that were difficult for her. A highlight of their visit was a trip to a village called Andrada in the Dundo area. The area had many independent churches but very little sound Bible teaching. Their plea was for missionaries to come and live among them, an echo of the call in the book of Acts, 'Come

---

6   2 Corinthians ch 12 v 9

over and help us'.[7] The visit was unforgettable, as Christians came together from five different places to greet them. There were so many that it wasn't possible to use the church building for a service, so Eric climbed on to the roof of the Land Rover and preached from there.

It was one of the few places in Angola that had both electricity and water, due to the influence of the diamond mine company, as well as a regular plane service. Ruth sent home a prayer letter after that visit, noting those facts, as a subtle reminder to anyone reading it that the 'sacrifice' someone would make in going there was much less than it would be anywhere else in the country.

Eric and Margaret's visit was a temporary one, for they had their own work to do elsewhere. So Ruth assessed the resources she had, which she could use to meet the needs of those at Saurimo who were also desperate for Bible teaching. The most important were the Emmaus Bible study correspondence courses she'd been working with since her earliest days at Biula.

---

7   Acts ch 16 v9

Chapter Ten

'Angelo angahi ali mwilu'
'How many angels in heaven?'

Cornwall, 2017

In the 'limbo' period between Ruth's diagnosis and the beginning of the treatment, she met up with Brian and Debbie at Weston-Super-Mare, and they spent the day together. Naturally they talked about Angola and the various aspects of the work there. One of those areas that Ruth had been involved with for many years, but which she had now handed over responsibility for to the Angolan staff, was the Emmaus work.

Angola: Emmaus Courses and Discipleship classes

To Ruth as a young and very new missionary, marking Bible study courses had felt like the most important task she fulfilled in her early years at Biula. The questions that students asked were interesting and varied, and sometimes amusing, for how could she answer the question 'How many angels are there in heaven?' She enjoyed the challenge of marking, and found the keenness of the students encouraging. However, it was impossible not to be moved when asked how many of the angels were black and how many white, a sad reflection of the all too real distinctions between peoples that were still apparent.

Even in the midst of the war, the Emmaus correspondence course work continued, with students sending in lessons from all over Angola, despite the difficulties of the unreliable postal service. Initially, the growth in popularity of the courses was due, in part at least, to the decline of atheistic Marxism and the consequent decrease in the persecution of professing Christians. But there were other factors at play, both positive and negative, as a result of the war. At Saurimo, in the war years, fewer folk from outlying villages could get into the town to bring Emmaus courses to be marked. This had been counterbalanced by an explosion of interest among those who fled from the villages. In town they had easy access to the courses, as well as more time on their hands. The net result was it was hard to keep pace with the demand. It was an enormous help to Ruth to have local volunteers step forward.

In 1998, towards the end of the war, the road from Saurimo to Lucapa opened again. Lucapa was a diamond town, 150 kilometres north, which resembled the 'wild west', and to be able to offer courses there was exciting. This time the problem in coping with demand wasn't the marking, but having sufficient supplies of the courses themselves. Some folk who couldn't get them complained Ruth was trying to stunt their spiritual growth! The cost of importing courses from Brazil and Portugal had increased, and many now wanted courses in Chokwe, as few outside the towns spoke or read much Portuguese. Translating courses was the first hurdle, printing them the second. It was a red-letter day at the Bible school building when a Risograph (a large-scale photocopier), booklet maker and collator arrived. Despite a few teething problems synchronising the booklet maker and the collator, printing courses locally significantly reduced the costs and ensured more folk could benefit from them. All they now needed were Angolan Christians to take on the practical aspects of the printing work. This role was filled first by Feliz and then by Jacob and has been a real spiritual benefit.

There was an additional problem with the Chokwe courses in that many Chokwes struggled with writing due to the lack of education during the war, thus deciphering their answers could be difficult. The benefits, though, far outweighed the problems. There were 317 men of varying ages studying in Chokwe and 225 young and literate men studying in Portuguese. One unintended consequence of having a team of young men to mark the courses was the challenge, for Ruth, when they came asking for advice on personal problems, such as marital issues, which she found difficult to answer as a single lady. Perhaps the most serious problem she faced was when one of her workers had to be suspended for adultery. He was repentant, but she had to tread a fine line between helping him to restore his marriage, while at the same time preserving the integrity and reputation of the Emmaus school. It left the other two workers carrying the load themselves. It was at times like these that dependence on and openness to God's guidance was most critical.

Ruth was aware that folk had different motives for doing the courses, some because they wanted a certificate, and some of those copied the answers to the questions from someone else who had already done them. But there were some who really appreciated them and read and re-read them, absorbing and living out what was taught. They were then able to share with others in their village churches, which was valuable as they might be the only person in their village who could read. These students made all the hard work worthwhile. However, at this stage there weren't any women taking the courses, and in order to address that problem Ruth invited an Angolan lady to become involved. The proportion of women taking courses gradually increased, though even today, twenty years after Paula first started working with Ruth, male students still outnumber females by ten to one.

With the end of the war, it was possible to open up regional centres for the marking of Emmaus courses, and as the number of students continued to increase, there was a need for a warehouse for storing the booklets. By 2009 a classroom and a library stocked with Bible study aids had been built, and by 2012 the work was completely in the hands of the Angolan staff, which had always been Ruth's aim. Four regional offices provided over fifty courses in Portuguese and fifteen in Chokwe, with the financial support of the newly formed Angolan Literature Fund. As well as production of the course books, it also financed the production of other copyright-free Christian literature.

In parallel with the Emmaus work, Ruth began discipleship classes, using courses sourced from Portugal, some at the Bible school and some in the churches around town. There were many young men interested in Bible study and it made such an obvious difference in their lives that some elders of the local churches came to Ruth asking if they too could be taught. Encouraged by their keenness to learn, she was distressed to discover at first hand how incomplete their knowledge was of even the basics of Christian doctrine. Their position as elders was due in part to cultural expectations and a lack of understanding of the Biblical qualifications of an elder. In Biblical terms, recognition of an elder should be based on spiritual maturity allied to a good reputation, rather than physical age or status within the community. In contrast, if a secular village elder became a Christian he was immediately expected to be recognised as an elder in the church also, regardless of his level of Biblical knowledge. That issue posed problems later for some of the young men whom Ruth had taught and who were ready to teach groups themselves.

By 1995 Ruth had fifteen groups in the various churches around town, and by 2001 two of her groups were nearing the completion of their courses. They had covered thirteen volumes over a period of ten years, and though they still needed some supervision, their discipline and dedication to studying the word of God was clear. They began to teach groups in their own churches. However, it was culturally inappropriate for a young man to show that he knew more than his elders. So, although elders were attending the groups and wanted to learn, those leading the classes struggled when it came to marking their work. One young man of about thirty was running a class in his church, which included two elders. He came to Ruth in distress, asking for advice. When he'd marked the first coursework, only two of the men had enough marks to pass, neither of whom were the elders. 'What can I do?' he asked. 'I can't fail them, they are elders.' It was a tricky situation to deal with, but the groups continued and the knowledge and understanding of all those studying increased.

As with any work for God there were both encouragements and discouragements. There were the young men who were working hard teaching groups faithfully, and there were those who fell away. Humanly speaking, they faced three main challenges as a result of their culture. The first was immorality – for the attitude to sexuality and to adultery was lax. The second was drunkenness – which was endemic in the society as a whole. And the third was witchcraft – which still had a hold on the majority of the population. Young Christian men and women were subject to these pressures daily and it was hard for Ruth to watch when someone who seemed so promising had to be disciplined by the church for succumbing to any of these temptations.

In these cases, she held on to the promise that God, who began a work in someone's life, would bring it to completion,[8] and she tried to look on these

---

8   Philippians ch 1 v 6

disappointments as a reminder of God's grace and patience with all Christians, missionaries included.

Nevertheless, the discipleship classes and the Emmaus work in Saurimo gave her great encouragement, for she saw it as building for the future, training young men to be the elders of tomorrow. One of her most important legacies to the churches in Chokweland is the young men who studied in her discipleship classes and have become the new generation of church leaders.

Sometimes problems came from an unexpected direction. The Bible Society stopped printing the 1970 version of the Chokwe Bible, although it was the bestselling Bible not only in Angola but also in the Congo and Zambia. Their new translation met with significant opposition all over Chokweland. The main problem was that it had been prepared in the Congo where Chokwe had become diluted through close connection with other languages. The Chokwes in Angola felt it would spoil the pure Chokwe of their children, so pleaded for it to be amended. When that request was refused, the elders in Saurimo formed a committee themselves to make suggestions for a revision of the 1970 version. By 1996 it was almost ready, and both the local missionaries and the Angolans were confident it would gain almost universal acceptance. The copies would be stored centrally and a pricing structure was agreed. All books, Bibles and hymn books were to be sold at cost plus transport. If any missionary felt that someone couldn't afford that, they should subsidise them from their own funds. It sold well in the towns, but so many folk in the villages couldn't afford it, Ruth had to find a way to make it accessible to them as well. Her immediate solution, though a bit of a hassle, was to trade Bibles for manioc, which she then sold in the market in town.

Emmaus and other Bible study courses and an affordable supply of Bibles met the need for those who were literate. However, schools in UNITA-held areas hadn't functioned since 1984, producing a generation who could neither read nor write but desperately wanted to learn. A quick survey showed literacy levels in churches in Saurimo were only 20 per cent, and levels in the country areas were much lower. Increasingly burdened, Ruth recognised she needed to make literacy a priority, for both adults and children. That was a long-term aim, but there were other ways of meeting the spiritual needs, particularly of the women.

Chapter Eleven

'Njeke ya loso'
'Packet soup and rice'

Cornwall, 2017

Sue and Colin Hares were among Ruth's many visitors at her house early in 2017. They were 'old' friends who dated back to her 'youth camp' days at Chy an Goon and Morthoe and had supported her both through prayer and also in practical ways during her years of service. Sue had visited her in Angola at a critical time when Ruth most needed physical help. They spent a pleasant afternoon sitting outside in her garden in the early spring sunshine reminiscing. Ruth had attended the camps both as a teenager and later as a young officer, and had entered fully into camp life. In team games, whether sport or otherwise, everyone wanted Ruth on their side, for her ability and fierce competitiveness was guaranteed to give them the edge. She was also renowned for her sense of fun and her inventiveness in practical jokes; most famously freezing a male leader's pyjama bottoms and running them up the camp flagpole. During a 'hunt the leader' competition in the nearby town, she and her best friend dressed up as elderly ladies, Ruth pretending to stagger along with a stick while pushing her friend in a wheelchair. They managed not to give the game away when she 'accidentally' tipped her friend out onto the pavement and passers-by rushed to lift her up again, but they both collapsed in fits of laughter as soon as they were out of sight. Fun aside, she was also very concerned for the campers' spiritual

growth, and she slipped away into her tent whenever there was a quiet mo-
ment to pray for those in her charge. Looking back, she saw how influential the
camps had been in her own spiritual development. It had been one summer, as
a teenager, while listening to a talk given by Peter Brandon, that year's camp
speaker, that Ruth first sensed that God might have a special job for her. She
had spoken to Peter about what she felt, and he had counselled her to tell no
one but wait to see what God would do. Never in her wildest dreams had she
imagined that God would send her to Angola in a time of war. One of the key
pieces in her 'jigsaw' of missionary work, both during the war and afterwards,
were women's 'camps'. The name was the same, but there the similarity to Chy
an Goon ended.

Angola: Women's work

One of the first things George Wiseman did when Ruth arrived at Biula was
to take her out to visit surrounding villages. There were many villages within
easy reach of the mission station. Small clusters of mud-brick houses, their
irregular thatched roofs alive with a myriad of creatures. She was struggling
to come to terms with them in her own room, but they didn't seem to bother
the locals. Flies were everywhere, and Ruth found herself constantly swat-
ting them away, but the women and children didn't appear to notice or be
irritated when they settled on their hair or their skin. She assumed, though
she found it hard to believe, that she would eventually get used to them too.
Outside each hut there was a cooking fire enclosed in a circle of loose stones,
the smoke curling upwards in thin spirals, the air pungent with the scent of
woodsmoke. Plastic basins held freshly harvested manioc tubers, or a few
tomatoes, or sweet potatoes, while all around scrawny chickens, followed by
their chicks, scratched and pecked at the dust. Cockerels strutted and crowed
and she heard the occasional bleat of a goat or sheep. She wondered what
any of the animals could find to eat on the parched earth between the huts,
and when she caught a glimpse of a goat, its ribs visible beneath its coat, it
was clear there would be little meat on the bones. Everywhere she went she
was moved by the women who pleaded with them to stay and hold meetings in their village, but George and Ena and Doris and Becky were already
overstretched. Some of the villages had a small hall where meetings could be
held; in others people sat under the trees for shade. Ruth desperately wanted

to be able to fulfil the requests of the many women and children who were so ready to listen, so redoubled her efforts to learn Chokwe. It was the key to being useful, for though Portuguese was Angola's official language, it was of little value in rural areas. Many adults in the villages had only a rudimentary understanding of it, if at all, the children, none. The ability to speak fluent Chokwe, their 'heart' language, was therefore essential.

In the following two years Ruth made good progress in language learning, though it felt frustratingly slow to her. She began by writing out short messages she could give, first to the children and then to groups of women, and gradually her fluency increased. When she moved to Luanda, she continued to focus on the Chokwe-speaking section of the population there, and by the time she relocated to Saurimo in 1989 she was fluent.

Most of the women's work in the north-eastern corner of Angola was done through what were termed 'camps'. Despite the name, rather than being residential, they were usually daily Bible schools, with the women returning home at night, unless the distance they had come was too great. Once every two months women from the churches in Saurimo came together on a Saturday for a full day of fellowship and teaching. When travel was possible, they were joined by women from the surrounding villages. The women themselves chose the topics to study. It was important to focus on topics that they felt relevant, which would help them in their everyday lives. It was easy to understand why they would want a study on marriage, or bringing up children, but some were more obscure and related directly to their cultural background. One such was the topic of 'Wednesday', or as it was called in Chokwe, the 'third day', for, following the period of communist rule, Monday was considered the first day of the week. The women were convinced that they should have a women's meeting at first light on Wednesdays, to imitate the women who ran to the tomb with spices on the third day to anoint Jesus's body after his death. Although Ruth and Mary often tried to explain that the third day after Jesus's death was actually Sunday – in Christian terms the first day of the week, the oral tradition of 'Wednesday' had continued, and so they agreed to make it a focus of a study day. It was an example of how important it was to be immersed in and understand the culture in which they worked in order to be truly effective.

Ruth held several camps at Saurimo during the war years, both for women and separately for young people and for children. Having sufficient food to provide even one meal a day for those who attended was a challenge. In 1995, in preparation for two camps, one for women, at which they expected 300, and one for young people, she took a trip to Luanda to pick up a ton of aid, including dry goods such as packet soup, and to buy sacks of rice and beans. It was hardly a varied diet, but it did at least mean everyone got something. Two years later, in 1997, the numbers attending a women's camp swelled to 500. Although trucks were beginning to go out to the villages to buy manioc, it was hard to get it in sufficient quantities, and also expensive. The beans she'd bought hadn't cooked properly, even after two days, so Ruth resorted once again to packet soup and rice. It was sobering to hear the topics some of the Angolan women chose to speak about at that camp – adultery, native medicine and fear of the spirits – clearly the issues that were impacting most on their lives at that time. At one camp after Ruth spoke, several women confessed their involvement with witch doctors and charms, and were thrilled to be reminded that God was greater than Satan.

Encouragements, such as the large numbers of women wishing to attend camps, were often counterbalanced by difficulties. Ruth wasn't surprised, for she understood that, alongside the physical issues she had to deal with, she was also fighting a spiritual battle. Towards the end of the civil war there was a new leadership team among the women, and though they were better educated than those who had gone before, Ruth felt their education was trumping a genuine desire to study the word of God. They'd organised a camp in her absence, choosing subjects such as the 'rights of women', rather than Biblical topics. Saddened, Ruth emphasised the importance of studying the word of God at every meeting and was pleased that for the next camp there was a return to Bible-based studies. The women faced so many pressures in running their homes and bringing up their children that it was difficult for them in their day-to-day living to devote time to studying God's word. In addition, the high levels of illiteracy meant that, for many, reading the Bible for themselves wasn't an option, so the time out at camp was vital.

It wasn't only the food that was a logistical problem, but also how to ensure the speakers could be heard above the clamour, especially of all the babies. In 2004, at a camp in Saurimo for 600 women, Ruth rigged up a loudspeaker powered by a small generator. It was fortunate she had access to one and the diesel to run it. Some of the women had no relatives in town, so needed to stay overnight, but although the Bible school dormitory had a roof, the floor wasn't cemented and there was no running water. It was a tribute to their commitment that many women still came and stayed, regardless of the physical conditions of their accommodation.

As the opportunities for travel opened up, Ruth travelled further and further afield, accompanied by some of the women from churches in Saurimo, to run camps or speak at women's conferences in areas that had been isolated for a long time. To get to one near Luau, they drove 300 kilometres, but when they got to the river, they found the bridge hadn't been repaired. They were thankful the water was shallow enough to wade across and walked the rest of the way to the village. It had been worth it to see 250 women from seventeen villages gathered there and have the privilege of teaching and encouraging them. The largest conference was one held near Biula, at which 3,000 women were present, coming from all over the area, including as far away as Luma Cassai. The need for Biblical teaching for women didn't diminish with peace, for as more and more goods became available, 'prosperity' doctrine began to gain ground. One speaker at a women's conference told the women that if they prayed like Hannah in the Old Testament,[9] 'salaries would be trebled and they would have wealth untold'. Ruth was incredibly saddened that some people failed to see that the only folk who became wealthy in these churches were the leaders. It was yet another area where it was vital that women got a good grasp of what the Bible actually taught on such matters, otherwise they would be disappointed in their faith.

Towards the end of Ruth's time in Angola, the pressures of work at the school at Camundambala meant that she couldn't sustain her own involvement in the women's work, but, as she'd always intended, the women she had taught and encouraged were continuing to teach and encourage others in their turn.

Cornwall 2016

When Ruth came home unexpectedly in December 2016, one very minor (and sadly temporary) indulgence she allowed herself was to buy her favourite sweets. Once she began her chemotherapy, she found that they increased her nausea and so she had to stop. She enjoyed wine gums and 'Skittles' and 'Shrimps' but her absolute favourite was a Sherbet dip dab. As she sat, dipping and licking, it

---

9   1 Samuel ch 1

reminded her of the hundreds, perhaps thousands, of lollipops she'd given out over the years to Sunday school children as prizes for memorising verses from the Bible.

Angola: Sunday Schools

With the prospect of peace, Ruth and Mary decided to tackle the issue of the huge numbers of young children who had little or no opportunity to learn what the Bible taught, in a way that was age appropriate. Of the eleven churches in Saurimo, only two had 'Sunday schools' and there were none in the villages. They held a 'seminar' (the 'buzz' word in government circles at that time, and thus in the churches also) setting out the advantages of Sunday schools, to inspire the church elders. The response was encouraging, and representatives from twenty-three village churches attended a practical seminar for prospective Sunday school teachers. One problem was that many of the villages had been attacked by UNITA and had scarcely a Bible or hymn book between them.

However, this initiative was successful, and by 2001 most of the town churches as well as some of the nearby villages and one of the refugee camps had a Sunday school. Ruth tried to get out to see them from time to time, but it was a challenge as they mostly met at 6.00 am! When they began, the children in the refugee camp had known nothing at all, not even the name of Jesus, for they had come from an area that had been under UNITA control for many years, with no access to any Bible teachers or preachers. It was a shock and a challenge, particularly for the lads who were helping Ruth, and illustrated both the scale of the needs and the exciting possibilities.

Gradually, over the next ten years, the Sunday school work developed and changed. She trained groups of young people, and on Sunday afternoons she would drive out, dropping them off in pairs at various villages and picking them up again afterwards to 'debrief' them. It was great for the children and useful training for the young people themselves. The children were enthusiastic and exuberant as they sang choruses, took part in quizzes and learnt memory verses from the Bible. Their pleasure, and that of the young leaders, was a delight to Ruth. Finally, in 2015, she was able to realise a long-cherished dream of a camp for Sunday school children led completely by Angolan young people. It was another milestone in her service, though she hadn't appreciated then how timely that handover of responsibility was.

Chapter Twelve

'Kuhona chinji Yitumbo yikehe'
'So much need, so few medicines.'

Cornwall

Ruth spent Christmas quietly with her family, apologising for 'gatecrashing' their celebration. As soon as possible afterwards she made an appointment with her GP and on the 13th January 2017 had an oncology appointment at Treliske hospital. She was given the diagnosis of an aggressive breast cancer. The speed and efficiency of the process of assessment and the access to appropriate treatment locally was in sharp contrast to the medical services available to the general population for much of her time in Angola.

Angola: Medical work

In areas of the world where there was little access to adequate medical care and treatment, medical work had traditionally been an important strand of mission. Biula was no exception. Ena and Becky were kept busy running the dispensary at the local hospital, providing training for local nurses as well as dealing with a large leprosy workload. There was no resident doctor, nevertheless, it provided a valuable service to the local population and a level of reassurance for the missionaries themselves. In Luanda there was little direct medical backup, though there were several clinics associated with other foreign missions. There was even less provision in Saurimo. The provincial government hospital was under-resourced, both in terms of personnel and medicines, and Angola, unlike the UK National Health Service, did not provide free treatment at point of need. Some oil and diamond companies had medical facilities, but these were generally reserved for the needs of their own employees. It wasn't until after the final peace that an Argentinian couple, who were both doctors, Juan and Adriana Palacio, came out to Luena to run an Angolan-built hospital there. In the periods when Ruth was alone at Saurimo during her last fourteen years, they were a valuable source of on the ground medical help and advice. Ruth had neither intended nor expected to be involved in medical missionary work, but faced with the desperate needs of a people whose lives were dominated by the consequences of war, she had no choice but to respond. It was one of many lessons in learning to live out the truth of Jesus' words: 'Whatever you did for one of the least of these brothers of mine, you did for me.'[10]

For many years Mary's clinic was one of the few sources of medicine in the whole of Lunda Sul province. It covered an area of 30,000 square miles, approximately the size of Scotland, so it was vital that it was kept going even when Mary was on a home visit or carrying out medical work elsewhere. Officially part of the provincial hospital, when left on her own, Ruth's role was simply to replenish the stock of medicine on a daily basis.

Though the diagnosis and commencement of Ruth's own treatment had been prompt and efficient, it wasn't entirely without problems. Following one of her chemo infusions Ruth was admitted to the hospital overnight and her post-chemo drugs were mysteriously 'lost' from a fridge in a controlled, staff-access-only room. It was thought that one of the staff had stolen them to sell, which for Ruth was a disappointing as well as painful reminder of a situation she'd battled against several times in Angola.

In 1992, in Saurimo, left in charge of the medical supplies, it hadn't taken Ruth long to realise that either the clinic was treating about 500 patients per day – which was impossible – or the nurses were siphoning off large quantities of medicine for resale.

---

10 Matthew ch 25 v 40

She understood the temptation for the Angolans – a nurse's salary was 9 million kwanzas per month, but despite the forthcoming elections and hope of peace, inflation was still rampant, a single egg costing a staggering 3 million kwanzas, and a bread roll 5 hundred thousand kwanzas. In contrast, the resale value of an aspirin on the black market was 1 million kwanzas, and a course of antibiotics, 60 million.

She tried to remonstrate, and to appeal for honesty, but in the end she had no alternative but to employ two Christians to dispense medicines from the front of her house until Mary returned. To close the clinic would have left the TB sufferers, as well as others who came looking for help, without any access to treatment, and would, inevitably, have resulted in increased illness and deaths within the community. The problem became even more acute in 1997 when, in the midst of ongoing conflict, Mary had to return to the UK for additional training and to have her own health monitored. Ruth was on her own for a year, attempting to juggle all her responsibilities – the Emmaus Bible study courses and discipleship classes for gifted young men and the literacy classes and Bible teaching for women – alongside Mary's medical work. When she found that the staff she'd employed were also stealing both medicines and money, she had to take over the dispensing herself until the church could provide her with more reliable workers. She'd found it stressful, unsure of what exactly to dispense and in what dose, but had to keep reminding herself that meeting physical needs was an essential strand of living out her faith.

At home during her early cycles of chemotherapy, Ruth started to have problems with the availability of medications. They were rarely in the pharmacy when they were due, which in turn impacted on the management of pain relief. She also had significant issues getting the pads she needed for her breast wound – nurses turned up at the house with a pad the size of a postcard, when one the size of a dinner plate was required. She commented philosophically to her brother, 'At least in England I can send you out to buy them. In Angola that wouldn't have been possible.'

In 1998 in Saurimo it had been even the most basic medicines, including streptomycin, a common antibiotic, and water for injections, which were in short supply. The situation was desperate – the clinic had very little medicine, the government posts had none, and the private post was beyond the means of most of the population. The health post in the large refugee camp was also desperate for help. They were convinced that many of the women and children they had in their feeding programme also had TB, but the local lab had run out of reagents to do the necessary diagnostic analysis. They felt it was pointless feeding people every day if they couldn't get medical aid for them. Ruth, galvanised by the possibility they might stop feeding needy people, began trading syringes with the military hospital to get needles and medicines in return.

And, as was so often the case in Angola, the problems seemed to multiply – the weather had been unkind, with non-stop rain, so that the mud bricks with which houses were built hadn't had time to dry out from one rainy season to the next. The result was that many houses had collapsed, and large numbers of people had been made homeless. Even in houses still standing, clothes and bedding were damp, so nearly everyone had a cough. The inability to test resulted in many being written up as TB patients. With the knock-on effect that precious TB medicine was used when it mightn't have been needed, and people who were misdiagnosed became resistant to the drugs. Despite the difficulties, Ruth didn't shut the clinic, but to ease the situation, she made the difficult decision to send new patients to a private clinic for testing regardless of the significant cost, in order to conserve the drugs they had.

Three years after the advent of peace, the stocks of medicines at the clinic in Saurimo remained an issue. By then it was possible to get supplies, the problem was the seeming inability of the helpers to think ahead or to correctly estimate the amounts required of a particular drug. When they came to tell Ruth they had no streptomycin, she couldn't understand why they hadn't requested it *before* it ran out, so she could get more in time. She found it frustrating that they had enough of some drugs to, in her words, '*last until the millennium*,' but they were never the day-to-day essentials. Some medicines they didn't need came in large quantities, while they received small amounts of others they did need. There were different medical needs and therefore different drugs required according to the time of year – for example, antimalarials and drugs for bronchitis were primarily needed between December and March, while in June and July the main problems were measles and scabies. But even that level of planning seemed beyond some of the helpers.

In the following years, though Ruth had been able to continue supplying beds and medicines for the various clinics, without Mary to oversee the clinic at Saurimo, staffing problems continued. A young man, whom Mary had sent to Luanda and paid for his training as a lab assistant, didn't want to come back to work unless he was guaranteed a house, a car and a salary of $600 per month – as much as local doctors earned. Ruth upheld the principle of paying staff a reasonable wage, but this disproportionate demand was a sobering illustration of how essential it was to ensure that anyone they involved in the medical work was also committed to doing it for the Lord, not just to 'get rich quick'.

Whatever the problems at Saurimo, there were plenty of encouragements in the expanding clinic work elsewhere. At Cavungo, near the Zambian border, there were two more clinics running, along with the new provision of ophthalmology. The medical posts at Biula and Luma Cassai were doing well, the leprosy village at Camundambala now had two trained nurses and a vaccinator, and the Palacios had taken over responsibility for Luena. Overall responsibility, however, still lay with Ruth, and she longed for someone who could take control of this aspect of the work.

By 2010 the main question was where and how medicines could be sourced most cheaply, as, due to high import duties, the containers from the UK that they'd depended on for so long were no longer economically viable. The wife of a short-term worker helped Ruth to do an audit of the various ailments which had been treated, and the drugs required. Not surprisingly, malaria and TB topped the list, with diarrhoea a close third. Of the many others, including anaemia, cholera and dysentery, most could be easily treated with the right drugs, or avoided entirely with access to clean water and better hygiene. It was another example of the need to blend in healthcare and training as an integral part of responding to the love she had experienced from God and, through expressing that love to others, to fulfil her primary 'call' – to draw them to Christ.

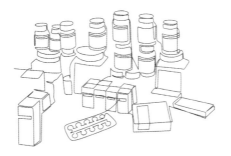

Chapter Thirteen

'Kachiki kaali muyisuho yiaali'
'There are two stages to malaria'

Cornwall, 2017

The 13th January 2017, the day Ruth received the news that the cancer they had found was aggressive, was the day she knew it would kill her. She had always been robust and physically strong, so her hope was that the plan – an MRI and bone scan, followed by eighteen weeks of chemotherapy and finally surgery – would allow her time, following the conclusion of the treatment, to return to Angola to conclude her work there and to pass it on to others in an organised manner. When she had first gone out to Angola aged twenty-six, she had been in good general health, but it didn't make her immune from disease, particularly those common to that area. It was something she had understood in principle before she took the decision to follow God's call, and she went prepared to take what precautions she could, and trust God for the rest. Over the next few months, in early 2017, as she attended the various appointments for assessments and treatment, she had time to reflect on the occasions in Angola when she or other of her missionary colleagues had been ill.

Angola: Missionary medical needs

Malaria is the disease most people associate with Angola – an ongoing problem, which Ruth and the other missionary personnel learnt to live with. Early in the 1990s she made light of it, writing that she was '...*keeping reasonably well, aside from occasional bouts of malaria.*' Some bouts, however, were more serious, a bad one often leaving her feeling very weak. In one of her typically semi-humorous asides in a letter home, she quoted Mary '*There are two stages to malaria – the first when you're afraid you'll die and the second when you're afraid you won't!*'

The entire province of Lunda Sul had been without supplies of antibiotics for five months, and had few other medicines. Ruth and Mary were particularly thankful for a containerload of medicines, both for the local population and for themselves. In Mary's case, one bout of malaria started from a cold and cough and developed into full-blown cerebral malaria. At that stage neither they nor the hospital had any quinine injections, but fortunately one of the nuns from the Catholic mission came, first to administer the injections, then returned to set up a quinine drip. Both Ruth and Mary had concerns about Mary's health, for she was often not very well. When she arranged to go home on furlough, but intended only staying for six weeks, Ruth felt she needed to take longer in order to have adequate health check-ups. With no medical training, Ruth felt inadequate to deal with a problem should one arise.

It wasn't an empty fear, for when Mary once again fell ill, Ruth and Eric and Margaret, who fortunately were with them, thought they might lose her. Mary, having recognised the symptoms of malaria, took a blood test, and in advance of a result – only available at night when there was electricity – dosed herself with quinine, which was the usual treatment. She seemed to be improving, but when Ruth went in to check on her later, she found her collapsed on the floor, semi-conscious, delirious, and not able to recognise anyone. They were fortunate to be able to get hold of a Bulgarian doctor, who thought her collapse was a reaction to the quinine and set up a drip, but because they had nothing to secure it with, he had to sit with his finger on the needle while the drip went in. Meanwhile, Eric held Mary's shoulders and Ruth her legs to stop her thrashing around. Ruth and Margaret sat with Mary in shifts until the morning, and by the following day she was stable, but the episode illustrated how vulnerable they all were. Without the Bulgarian doctor they wouldn't have had any idea how to cope.

The problems arising from the scarcity of local medical care weren't solved by peace. Although Angola had a wealth of natural resources in the form of oil and diamonds, the money didn't filter down to the people. Hospitals were built but not staffed, and medicine remained in short supply. In September 2003 Ruth had a meal in a village, which had been cooked the previous day. As a result of the heat and the lack of refrigeration, it had grown either E.coli or salmonella. This was immediately followed by a urinary tract infection and topped off by malaria. The combination made her very ill, but fortunately Mary was there at the time. She took Ruth to a hospital in a diamond town north of Saurimo, and having got treatment and medicines, she cared for her at home. There was a long way to go before anyone, including missionaries, would have the sort of healthcare that we take for granted.

The following month, Ruth was once again alone and suffered a fever which progressed to numbness and tingling in her fingers and pain in her wrist and thumb. Aside from the discomfort, it made it difficult to do the most basic tasks – carrying water, filling the generator with fuel, and so on. There was no one she could consult locally, and when there was no improvement after almost six weeks, she was sufficiently concerned to try to set up a phone call with Ian Burness, a former missionary doctor based in the UK, to chat through her fevers. The sensible option was to return home for proper assessment and treatment. Obvious, but not easy to achieve, as the runway at Saurimo was shut for repairs and therefore closed to commercial flights, and the nine-hundred and forty-five-kilometre drive to Luanda was impossible with the condition of her hands. When a World Food Programme plane *was* allowed to land, she was able to pay for a passage to Luanda on its return journey. Economy class on British Airways isn't wonderfully comfortable, but it certainly beats sitting among crates on a cargo plane. Ruth had travelled that way many times before, so her overwhelming feeling was gratitude for the timing of the flight, which once again she saw as God's answer to her prayer. Once home, after an urgent neurological appointment impossible in Angola, she was diagnosed with severe nerve compression (carpal tunnel syndrome) in her right wrist, and moderate in her left, explaining the lack of feeling in her fingers. The consultant's opinion was that it was a result of the fevers and the cocktail of medicines she had taken, so it should die down itself, rather than require surgery. After a follow-up appointment towards the end of November she was cleared to return.

Later, in October 2009, Ruth was once again alone and unwell but didn't know what was wrong. She treated herself for malaria first, and when that made no difference, she took a general antibiotic. Her symptoms were a general lethargy, lack of stamina, nausea, a feeling of being full as soon as she ate even the smallest amount of food, jaundice and an inability to drink tea. That was a definite sign that something was very wrong, as her norm was ten to twenty cups per day! She thought of going to consult the Palacios at Luena. Though it was a long journey, she wanted to visit Biula and Luma anyway, so it would've made sense to go on from there. First, however, she once again contacted Ian Burness. Based on her reported symptoms, he suggested she might be suffering from Hepatitis B and recommended lots of rest, liquids, fruit and sugar. Anything milky or fatty would increase the nausea and probability of being sick. That wasn't good news, on several counts. Rest was almost impossible to achieve and it meant she couldn't eat chocolate, one of the treats she looked forward to when a container arrived. She would hoard and dispense it to herself as if it were medicine (which, as anyone who enjoys chocolate knows, it almost is). If she didn't improve quickly she thought she might have to bring forward her home trip. In the meantime, in case word had leaked out that she was ill, she wrote to her home church: '*I'm writing to let you know I'm not about to kick the bucket...*'

By November, when Jonathan and Ruth Singleton arrived on a short-term visa, she was feeling significantly better but still lacking in stamina. She found her weakness frustrating when there was so much work needing to be done, but fortunately Jonathan and Ruth were able to take on a lot of her responsibilities. She decided not to bring her furlough forward but to go home as planned in December and get a thorough check-up then. By this stage she was able to eat normally and expected to be back to full strength soon, but in a typical flash of humour, she thought maybe she should look at the list of jobs she'd like done *before* she admitted to improvement.

It wasn't only illnesses that were an issue, accidents were equally problematic. Ruth was fortunate that she only suffered two potentially serious accidents during her entire time in Angola. The first was in 1987. Throughout most of her years of service, particularly during the war and its aftermath, Ruth, in common with the other missionaries, relied heavily on the containers of aid sent out from the UK. They came into the port, and once the paperwork was complete and the fairly hefty fees were paid, it was released. When one arrived with a car and other goods, she headed out to Viana on the outskirts of Luanda with Charlie Shorten to try to straighten out one of the doors on an old container they used for storage until stuff could be shipped inland. In the process she crushed three fingers on her right hand and severed the top of her little finger. Their first thought was to contact a Brazilian missionary to ask if it would be possible to go to the hospital owned by the Brazilian company Gamek, but they couldn't get through to him. Then they remembered a British doctor was visiting, so phoned him. He could stitch the top of her finger back on but had no suture material nor anaesthetic, and Ruth wasn't wanting to let anyone within a mile of her finger without it. He suggested the Swiss Reformed Church clinic might have what was needed, so they rushed there, catching the nurse with five minutes to spare. By this time the top of her finger was turning black, so the doctor wasn't hopeful it would 'take' but stitched it back on anyway. Even a shot of morphine didn't suppress the pain sufficiently to let Ruth sleep, and when the stitches came out a few days later, half of the finger was still black. The doctor who stitched her finger back on had already left the country, so there was no one she could consult.

She didn't know what to do, other than keep it bandaged, but when she happened to go to the Brazilian hospital to visit an in-patient, the nurses, having asked her what she'd done, insisted on taking a look. They were so horrified they called a doctor, who called another one and then a third. It was Ruth's turn to be horrified when they suggested amputation, but they finally agreed to dress and clean it daily for two weeks to see if it could be saved. Fortunately, by then it looked sufficiently improved that they decided amputation would probably not be necessary – much to Ruth's relief.

God isn't a magician who miraculously protects from accidents all those who follow him. But He has promised 'In all things God works for the good of those who love Him, who have been called according to His purpose.'[11] For Ruth, this event illustrated the truth of that promise, as she now knew they could go to the Brazilian hospital in an emergency. And in addition, the Brazilian staff were so astounded she was in Angola without proper medical backup that she was able to share God's call on her life and the message of the gospel with them. It was also a lesson in patience – not Ruth's strongpoint – as even after a month she couldn't drive the car that had come out in

---

11 Romans ch 8 v 28

the container, for she couldn't grip the steering wheel or change gear. On the plus side, it gave her a welcome rest from the washing up, an opportunity to be looked after by the others, and time to read – a treat often reserved for her short home visits. Reading about the problems and issues the missionary Amy Carmichael faced in India, some one hundred years earlier, helped her to see that the frustrations and problems she was encountering were by no means unique, and the same God who sustained Amy Carmichael would sustain her too.

Twenty-six years later, in 2013, eleven years after peace had finally come to Angola, Ruth had her second potentially serious accident. Little had changed in terms of medical provision. The only major difference was that she now had medical insurance. These days it is considered normal, possibly even mandatory, but that wasn't the case when she first went out in 1982. She'd had a few falls in her time, mostly near misses with only minor damage, but this time, falling as she tried to chase a couple of drunks out of the back of her vehicle, she damaged her ankle. By now Saurimo boasted a private clinic, and she went there to consult the Romanian doctor. He wanted X-rays, but, predictably for Angola, even in a private facility in peacetime, he hadn't enough X-ray material to get all the angles he required. From what he could see he thought it was dislocated, but as the private clinic didn't do plastering, she was sent to the government hospital, where she was put in a back slab and told to come back in six weeks. Once again, it was fortunate she had visitors staying who could help out. However, when she telephoned, both Ian Burness in the UK and Sam Simonyi-Gindele, the missionary doctor now at Biula, both recommended she went home for a proper diagnosis and treatment, as they felt it was unlikely she would have dislocated her ankle without a fracture. It wasn't possible to take an internal flight with the back slab, so Ruth had a rather uncomfortable seventeen-hour car journey to Luanda and flew home accompanied by Sue Hares and Sue Edgeler, who were able to help at the airports. Once home, it was confirmed that her ankle was broken and required to be screwed and plated. It is only when she was back in Angola that she realised how much she walked and stood, and how uneven the terrain was – a wee bit of a struggle with her now weakened ankle.

In February and March 2017 Ruth underwent successive rounds of chemotherapy. They followed the normal three-week cycle. To begin with she reacted much as expected – initially totally floored, a gradual improvement in stamina in the middle week, and then a 'good' week, before the next infusion. As the treatment progressed, her levels of tiredness increased, along with what she termed her 'brain fog'. For someone who was used to being able to keep lots of different 'balls' in the air at one time, it was a wee bit frustrating to find her mind wasn't as sharp as she was used to.

She didn't suffer from 'brain fog' at any stage of her time in Angola, but she did admit to recurring periods of extreme tiredness and even exhaustion. It was in the spring of 1998 she suffered her first protracted period of extreme tiredness. She went home for a very short visit to check if her thyroid or some other condition was at fault, or if it was just 'her age'. Six years later, when she was in her mid-forties, she once again mentioned getting tired very easily, this time querying whether it was her age or a case of trying to do too much. Undoubtedly, she did do too much, something both she and others recognised, but often there was little alternative. She would be on the go from early morning until late at night, and particularly once Camundambala school was up and running, she would be there from 7.30 am till at least 5.00 pm, often teaching classes as well as running the school. When she returned home in the evening she found a queue of people outside her door, all re-quiring her help or advice. Most nights it was 7.00 pm before she had sorted everything and sometimes as late as 9.00 pm. Which was much too late to think of cooking supper.

Towards the end of her time, one of her Angolan workers insisted she get some help in the house, realising that otherwise she might go for days without proper food. It was something she'd always resisted, as she didn't want to fall into the trap, or even the appearance, of 'white colonialism'. She was aware that, despite the poor quality of her house and living conditions by Western standards, it was far superior to that of many of the Angolans she worked among and alongside. In the end, however, she accepted it was a necessity.

The war years were particularly problematic, especially when the fighting was nearby, with the additional stress of imminent danger. That was phys-ically draining, as was carrying out work for which she didn't feel mentally equipped. Sometimes, though, her tiredness could be explained by the sheer volume and variety of work she shouldered, particularly at times when she was on her own. Aside from teaching every day and supervising building work, she was also taking overall responsibility for the Emmaus Bible study work, the lepers in the village at Camundambala, and the maintenance of all the mission buildings, not just at Saurimo and Camundambala, but at other places also. At one point she had to halt the building work temporarily as she didn't have time to go to buy materials. They had run out of blocks and big bolts for the roofing joists and she needed to scour Saurimo at every mechanics' yard. Another important contributory factor was the difficulty of getting regular trips home and the impossibility of taking breaks within the country. On one occasion, knowing she couldn't get out, a friend suggested she should take a holiday locally. Ruth's response was, '*Where could I go and who could I go with?*' It was a legitimate question, for there was nowhere to go and no one available to accompany her.

Because of the amount of work she did, the weight of all the responsibilities she carried and the stresses of the local situation, the mission organisation which channelled funds to her (at that time known as Echoes of Service, now Echoes International) suggested she should attempt to get home for a short period each year. It wasn't always possible, though in her latter years she did try to come home at some stage during the Angolan school holiday period. She did also manage a couple of trips into Zambia to visit missionaries there and had one memorable holiday when some of her family came out to visit and she took them over the border in order to see some African wildlife, which had been missing from Angola since the start of the war.

Twice more she wrote of extreme exhaustion, and in 2015, when she was almost sixty, having had four weeks of constant cold, flu, a cough and then malaria, she reckoned it was warning that she needed to cut back. Her aim had always been to work herself out of a job by equipping local Christians to progressively take over her various roles and she had hoped to retire at the age of seventy, but God had other ideas.

Chapter Fourteen

'Musongo wa a Chokwe, hi wa Zambi ko'
'An illness of the Chokwes, not of God'

Cornwall, 2016

On Ruth's last furlough, it was impossible to avoid Halloween. For weeks the shops were full of 'Halloween' merchandise – bins of giant pumpkins in every supermarket, the clothing aisles packed with skeleton outfits, demon costumes complete with horns and forked tail and red plastic tridents, witches' pointy hats, vampire cloaks and printed masks with sharp teeth and trails of blood. It seemed that every year the costumes became more lurid. Even common sweets had seasonal versions – themed for Halloween in orange and red and black. For Ruth, it was impossible to be bombarded by these images, which trivialised witchcraft and the spirit world, without thinking of what it meant for Angolans.

Angola: Witchcraft

The medical problems Ruth and the other missionaries faced were primarily physical issues. But for the Angolans there was an added, and very disturbing dimension, often with extremely serious consequences. The lack of medicines in Lunda Sul province had caused a resurgence of witchcraft practices. The Chokwe culture taught that any illness or accident must be caused by some-one, and therefore it was the responsibility of family members to find out who was responsible, so that blame could be apportioned and retribution carried out. For Christians who had relatives who weren't Christians, or were only nominally Christian, there was tremendous pressure to consult the diviner when illness struck. Ruth recounted the story of an elder in one church who had been admitted to hospital with TB. After a week his family took him from the hospital and consulted a diviner before taking him to a witch doctor. The diviner said his uncle and grandmother were to blame, and so the grandmother was beaten to death and the uncle poisoned. The witch doctor then said the patient would die, and sure enough, three hours later he did. It was a tragic loss of life that wouldn't have happened had he continued with treatment in the hospital.

Even more tragically, the half of the family who were Christians didn't understand Ruth's horror at what had happened. Their feeling was that they had purged society of two assassins. Though they knew that God forbade divining, their excuse was that this was a '*Musongo wa a Chokwe, hi wa Zambi ko*' (an illness of the Chokwes, not of God). It was a tangible sign of the fear of witchcraft that still had a hold over the local people, even those who claimed to be Christian. And it indicated how hard it was for older generations, particularly, to break free from the negative aspects of their culture. Ruth never had any desire to turn anyone into Westerners, and respected and admired much of their culture – their resilience, their friendliness, their hospitality, even their brashness, which she found easy to relate to – but to see them bound by fear was heartbreaking. It was also a sobering illustration of how difficult it was to combat this fear without sufficient clinically trained personnel and an adequate supply of medicines, validating the importance of medical missionary work.

However uncomfortable we in the West are, and however hard we find it to accept that these problems still exist, it is a reality for the Chokwe people.

On one occasion Ruth went to a village north of Saurimo with an Angolan elder. She was to speak to the women and the elder was to do a Bible study with the men. As was often the case when someone new came to a village, the villagers spent a lot of time singing and greeting. While Ruth smiled and greeted and waited, she saw a little girl standing in the doorway of a house whose face and arms were white, indicating she was ill and being treated with traditional medicine. Moved, Ruth spoke to the women about a verse from the New Testament – 'The one who is in you, is greater than the one who is in the world.'[12] Later they were invited to the local elder's house and found it was the same one where Ruth had seen the little girl. After a meal the elder brought forward his daughter, who now had no visible whitening on her, and asked if Ruth had any medicine for her. Ruth hadn't, but she suggested he bring the child to Saurimo and she'd see what she could do there. And then to encourage them to put their trust in God rather than the witch doctor, she said they'd pray for the girl and turned to the visiting elder expecting him to do so. To her astonishment he refused, and so Ruth prayed for the girl herself. As they drove away, she asked the elder why he wouldn't pray. His answer was a sad commentary on the culture of fear in Chokwe society – 'If I had prayed and the child didn't get better, they would accuse me of bewitching her. Better that *you* pray.'

In November 2013, thirty years after first coming to Angola, she wrote an article which opened:

> *You don't have to live for very long in Central Angola before you realise the all-dominating, pervasive factor is a crippling and en-slaving fear of witchcraft. Witches (and sorcerers) are perceived to be a threat to the harmony and balance of relationships in a community, and thus are the most hated people in Angolan society. In Angola and in particular among the Chokwes, those accused of witchcraft are often beaten to death, which is seen as a service to the community, in much the same way that we would be relieved when someone guilty of murder is jailed for life.*

The prevailing (and appropriate) view that Western missionaries shouldn't try to replace native cultures with their own was a principle that Ruth firmly upheld. However, witchcraft in Angola cannot be trivialised, as it often is in Western cultures. It is a very real and evil influence on people and society which often leads to violence and death. Sometimes missionaries from the West have belittled it as ignorant superstition, and thus are of little use or help to the local Christians who are battling with the tremendous family and social pressures which arise from a belief in the malign power of spirits. On the other extreme, some have reinforced its power and influence by holding witch hunts within the churches and claiming to have cast out demons. Ruth

---

12 1 John ch 4 v 4

was totally convinced both of the reality of the belief in and fear of witchcraft and witchcraft practices, and that it was only the power of God which could release people from their fear. In case you think this is something that might have been true in previous centuries but no longer applies, Ruth's personal experiences right up until she had to leave Angola in 2016 show otherwise.

Her first experience of witchcraft was just six months after her arrival in 1982, when she witnessed two elderly people being beaten to death. Again and again over the intervening years she saw the problems her Angolan Christian friends and co-workers faced due to the prevailing belief in witchcraft. She recounted many examples, though I have space for only a few.

While riding his motorbike, her best worker had an accident and knocked over a child, who then died. Although the accident wasn't his fault and all those who witnessed it testified to his innocence and the authorities likewise absolved him of all blame, he was forced out of Saurimo due to accusations of witchcraft and threats of vengeance from the child's family.

One of the elders in a village church was accused of witchcraft and the king of the area shut the church down. A few months later a church building was knocked down in another village because the villagers had accused one of the leaders as 'having witchcraft'. She would have liked to help the Christians in that village rebuild, although it would have had to wait for the dry season, but it was unlikely that such help would be welcomed, as the villagers would be afraid to be associated with the person accused.

A village chief who had been put out of his church for divining and worshipping idols started targeting the church elders. He beat one man to death, and another was forced by the diviner to drink the poison cup, leaving the remaining elders afraid of who might be next. The son of the man killed found it hard to stay in the village, especially as the authorities couldn't or wouldn't do anything to bring the chief to justice.

Towards the end of her time in Angola she noted, with sadness, that even Christians, who once might have hidden their fears from missionaries, now talked of them openly, seemingly without any sense that these attitudes and fears were inappropriate. Just as with illness, any misfortune – an accident, crop failure, or the loss of a job – could be attributed to witchcraft, with the consequent need to find a scapegoat to blame. It was another sign that often in this corner of north-eastern Angola a ritual to the Great God (Zambi) had simply been added to all the other rituals, rather than replacing them.

Even more discouraging, elders at a church conference suggested that an accusation of witchcraft against anyone by a diviner should result in them being barred forever from church membership, implying that all accusations had validity, when the reality of course was most had not.

She continued:

> *If you work in clinics, every day you see professing Christians coming in with all sorts of things tied around their waists. In school the children have things on their wrists and ankles and around their necks to protect them. We cut them off when we can. There are some believers who don't wear them, but I would be afraid to say someone is delivered (from a belief in and fear of witchcraft), because although they may not have divined for a while, it's possible their family have been healthy. As soon as a child or grandchild gets ill then they may go to the diviner, and if they don't go themselves (as they don't want to be put out of the church) they may pay for their family to go and divine. Few believers, even seemingly the strongest, are able to stand up against witchcraft accusations, and most under torture, even though innocent, will confess.*

However, she was encouraged when she thought of individuals who courageously refused to bow to the prevailing atmosphere. One teacher went from class to class telling the children of the power of God to protect them and cutting off the supposedly protective red bands on each child's wrist. A lady refused to divine when her husband suffered a stroke. One of her workers who, when his wife and then his daughter died, refused to believe the accusations made against his brother or to ostracise him. These and many others were chinks of light in the darkness.

Chapter Fifteen

'Ola ya Angolano'
'Angolan time'

Cornwall, 2017

In many countries there are cultural differences between regions. Even neigh-
bouring counties may have distinct traditions they hold to, sometimes fiercely.
This is particularly important in the 'Celtic fringe' of the UK, of which Cornwall
is part. On Ruth's birthday in February 2017, her brother took her for a day
out, culminating in an afternoon 'cuppa' in Gwithian. Unfortunately, as it was
out of season, they weren't able to have a traditional Cornish cream tea but
had to make do with just the tea. It was a real disappointment to miss out on
a scone spread with jam and a generous dollop of cream on the top. Had they
strayed into neighbouring Devon they would have been offered a scone spread
with cream and jam on the top. The residents of both counties are adamant
their way is the 'right' one. Sometimes it is understanding the details, the little
things, that mark someone out as 'belonging'.

Angola: Culture

In Ruth's time in Angola she had come to understand and appreciate much
of Chokwe culture, evidenced by the fact that many of the Chokwes I interviewed for this book told me Ruth was 'one of us' and Chokweland was her

'home'. She had been in north-eastern Angola for so long she admitted to thinking in Chokwe, and struggled sometimes to express herself in English. That's not to say she didn't make mistakes, or on occasions offend people, but she made the effort to delve deep into their culture and it paid off.

There were aspects of Chokwe culture that she found attractive right from the very beginning. Chokwes' homes were always open, a welcome was guaranteed and they were always willing to share what they had, however little that might be. When a visitor came they would give them a gift, even when it would leave themselves with nothing. Ruth learnt quickly that it was important to take whatever was offered, for to refuse it, even with the best intention, would have caused offence. As a result, even during the war years, when everyone was struggling for food, Ruth was careful to accept hospitality, but equally careful to eat as little as possible, so as not to leave the host with nothing. And wherever and whenever possible to share what she had also.

In Angolan church services, Ruth experienced 'Angolan time' – the first thirty minutes at least after the official start time devoted to singing, to allow for the congregation to drift in in ones and twos, only beginning properly once enough people had arrived. Most people enjoy singing, or at least listening to it, and as the Chokwes have a natural ability to harmonise, the singing was uplifting, though the delay could sometimes be frustrating. Similarly, on arrival at a village, for example to speak to the women, it was important not to 'rush' the greetings, but to allow for a lengthy period of 'welcoming' which could include both singing and a telling of everything that had happened during the day, before starting the main purpose of the visit. While Ruth's natural character was to 'get on with the job', she learnt patience and came to appreciate the sentiment behind the lengthy greeting process.

Some aspects of the local culture initially seemed to be similar to her own but were actually the result of a whole different way of thinking. It was vitally important to understand, not just how things were worked out in practice, but also the underlying belief system. When a relative of someone from the UK dies while abroad, for example on holiday, it is usual to bring the body home for a funeral. Similarly, she discovered it was very important for Angolans to be buried on their home territory. When a Christian, who came from Saurimo but was studying in Lubango, died suddenly, leaving a wife and four children, the Christians in Lubango were trying to get his body home. Not easy nor inexpensive in the midst of a civil war. However, it wasn't just a case of a family wanting to have a grave or memorial to be able to visit, or to experience what we in the West call 'closure'. Although his widow was a believer, many of his family were not, and they were afraid that if he wasn't buried at home he would come back to haunt them as they hadn't properly laid him 'to rest'. Although Ruth understood the background and the difficulties, it raised a dilemma for her. She didn't want to reinforce the superstition, but as his wider family weren't Christians, she didn't want to antagonise them either. It was one of many complex decisions she had to make over the years.

She faced another culturally driven dilemma in the medical work. On one occasion a man came requiring medicine for a particular condition. As Ruth had nothing appropriate in the clinic, she once again sought the advice of Ian Burness. He would be able both to prescribe and to send out a drug to help. He mentioned two drugs – a 'best' drug in terms of the condition, but which carried the culturally difficult side effect of reducing libido. And a 'second best' drug which could impact on blood pressure. In the UK, if it was affordable, the 'best' drug would have been offered, with appropriate warnings about the potential side effects, but the situation was more complex in the Angolan culture, where virility was of primary importance. There the 'second' best might be preferable to the patient.

Chokwes clap to welcome someone who visits them. It isn't applause, it's a way of indicating their pleasure at seeing the visitor. But sometimes seemingly minor differences are symptomatic of serious underlying beliefs and thinking and it is important to be able to distinguish which is which. The clapping has no sinister undertones, but a handshake may have. In the UK and many other countries, holding out one hand to shake is the norm. For a Chokwe, a single hand held out in greeting, with the other hidden, could be concealing evil intent. Holding out both hands showed openness and friendship. This was one example of the background of superstition that Ruth found still had a hold on many, particularly among the older generation.

There were other aspects of the Chokwe psyche that she found even more challenging. There are many tribal groups in Angola, but the three main ones were the Umbundu, the Kimbundu and the Chokwe. Of these, the Chokwe were perhaps the most proud and most arrogant. They didn't ask for something, they demanded it, and expected to get it. Some of the men who knew Ruth best, and who had worked with her the longest, talked of 'teaching her our culture' but mentioned how difficult she found it to relate to and accept this 'demand' culture. For Ruth it implied a feeling of inappropriate entitlement, especially when it was fellow Christians doing the demanding. When she was going home for a short visit, some folk demanded that she would bring them back lots of books, and were taken aback when she said, '*I'm only allowed twenty kilos, how do you expect me to bring back all this?*' While she applauded their desire for good Bible study material, she found it frustrating that they seemed to have no conception of how little could be carried in the twenty-kilogramme luggage limit and that there might be things she needed to bring back herself. The 'I want and I should get' attitude was guaranteed to make her cross, right up to her final days in Angola, along with folk complaining, particularly about others, which often led to her 'exploding' at the person in question.

Cultural understanding is a two-way street, and her closest Chokwe friends and colleagues learnt how to moderate their interactions with Ruth in order to achieve their desired end. As one of her co-workers put it, 'You needed to be clever, and subtly mention your need in conversation, not as a direct demand. A comment such as, "We don't have any food in our house today" would immediately produce a positive response'. Many reported that although Ruth could 'blow up' in an instant, she also calmed down quickly, never held a grudge and, more importantly, if she was in the wrong, she apologised. Sometimes the apology was necessary because she'd blown up at something very trivial as a result of other pressure. Recognising the burdens of responsibility she carried and the level of stress she was often under, when she came to apologise and explain, they would say, 'Don't worry, we understand.'

One of her teacher colleagues told me the story of when he'd been in the 'firing line'. She was paying his salary herself, as he wasn't government funded. When she went on furlough, she left instructions for Brian and Debbie to continue paying him, but unfortunately she made a mistake in the amount she told them to pay, doubling his salary. When she came back and recommenced paying him, she gave him what he'd been paid before. He asked why he wasn't getting the increased salary, and Ruth, not realising it had been her own mistake, reacted angrily and, in his words, 'made him feel like a thief.' Later, when she saw she was in the wrong, she took him aside and apologised, and continued to pay the higher salary. As he shared his story, over five years later, the positive impact of that apology was still apparent. He had been astounded that Ruth, as a white person, would be sufficiently humble to admit her mistake and proffer an apology. In a way it had been of more value to him than the money had been, for it raised his self-esteem.

However, it was both a sad reflection of his initial sense of lesser worth, undoubtedly a hangover from the colonial era, and an encouragement, that it was possible, by behaving properly, to overcome that legacy.

She didn't blow up in every context. When I questioned her closest colleague in the Emmaus work, she said that she'd heard others talking about Ruth 'exploding' but had never experienced it herself. Which was perhaps a reflection of the fact that the Emmaus work, though often demanding in terms of time and energy, was rarely frustrating or emotionally exhausting. In the schools, she led by example and taught the teachers that they should never shout at the children but rather seek to encourage them, even when discipline was necessary. One amusing example of this combination was how she dealt with a boy who described himself as a 'bandit', who didn't want to go to school. Ruth recognised that he was capable of learning but didn't have any motivation. So at least two or three times a week she would go to the leper village to his house to bring him to school when he didn't come himself. Even at that, she'd have to give him sweets or biscuits to get him in the door. If he was very naughty during school she would lock him out, but she would arrive to collect him again the next day. Without her persistence he wouldn't have passed through school. Nor have his current job, a valued worker at Camundambala.

Two aspects of culture that continued to upset and frustrate Ruth throughout her ministry were the Angolan attitude to teenage pregnancies and the valuing of 'form' over 'substance'.

Pregnancy before marriage wasn't considered a problem, even among some professing Christians, but rather a helpful proof of the girl's fertility. The net result were many teenage pregnancies, so that when Ruth established schools after the end of the war, it wasn't unusual to have very young, unmarried girls trying to study while pregnant, or with a small baby. Ruth was concerned to provide teaching to them on the importance of chastity and marriage, both from a religious and an educational and social point of view. So she ran a girl's camp focusing on this topic. One head teacher that Ruth appointed made a rule that if a girl fell pregnant she couldn't stay at school. Initially this worried Ruth because she felt too many girls would lose out on education, but she changed her mind when the rate of teenage pregnancies fell dramatically. Ruth, coming from the West, would have preferred a 'carrot' approach, while the local head teacher understood that culturally a 'stick' approach was more likely to get results.

Frequently, for a Chokwe, what was visible was more important than what was actual. For example, churches were full on Sundays with worshippers who gave every appearance of spirituality, yet often their Monday to Saturday lives were dominated by immorality, witchcraft and drunkenness, all of which were incompatible with a profession of faith. They seemed to work on the principle that if inappropriate behaviour was hidden, it didn't matter. They aren't alone in that, of course. Sadly, it happens in churches in many other countries too – hypocrisy is a charge often made against Christians. Perhaps the distinction in Angola was the scale of the problem. It was certainly an issue Ruth battled against on a regular basis.

Chapter Sixteen

'Kangonga ni vula munji'
'Fierce storms and monsoon rains'

Cornwall, 2017

Ruth leaned on the window ledge in her lounge in St Austell in January 2017 and watched the rain pelting against the glass. She could hear the wind in the branches of the trees on the roads above and below the cul-de-sac in which her house stood. They bent and swayed, their low moaning penetrating the double glazing. She was glad she didn't have an hospital appointment, for watching the rain from the warmth and comfort of inside was one thing, being out in it would be less pleasant. But however hard it rained, there was little danger of the house suffering serious damage. Aside from the (thankfully rare) severe weather events, winter might bring down the odd loose slate, or the gutter might overflow, but that would be all. It would be raining in Angola too, but the destructive impact on traditionally built houses wasn't just likely, but almost inevitable.

Angola: Building work

All year round the Angolan traditional mud or burnt brick buildings were vulnerable to the ravages of termites, and so the need for regular rebuilding was normal. In the rainy season, when they could least afford a building to be damaged, as building or repairs were almost impossible, they were vulnerable to extremes of weather: fierce storms could rip off thatched roofs and torrential monsoon rains could cause walls to collapse, or wash them away.

A year after Ruth's arrival at Biula, Roy Wood, a former missionary, came to undertake all the necessary repairs on the mission station houses. Among the other building and renovation jobs, he replaced the thatch on Ruth's room with asbestos sheeting. It was a welcome goodbye to creatures running around above her head at night, though had she known anything of the dangers of asbestos, she might not have been so happy. As it was, she was blissfully ignorant of any potential hazard. She was given the task of driving a team of men out to cut timber for roofing the new garage, and for the building work proposed for the following year. It was twenty kilometres to the river Kende where the trees were tall and straight and perfect for the job, and though she didn't know it then, the driving back and forwards was a small foretaste of the transportation of building materials and men that she would do many times over the next thirty-three years.

It wasn't only houses that required constant maintenance, upgrading or replacement. Church buildings of mud-brick construction were equally vulnerable and, due to their larger scale, harder to work on. She remembered being in a church service at Saurimo, towards the end of the 1990s, when the roof blew off and a wall fell in, injuring several people. One elder had crush injuries to his legs and a young man crushed vertebrae (or something similar). Without an orthopaedic specialist to check him over it was difficult to know exactly what the problem was. Whatever the diagnosis would have been, he was unable to move his legs, though he did have 'pins and needles', which they all hoped was a positive sign. As usual, the hospital didn't have the materials to put him in plaster, and all that Mary could do was provide some painkillers while the whole church prayed for his recovery. Nothing at all could be done for the building until the dry season came.

When Ruth's mum died, the house she'd been living in, and which Ruth had come home to when she was on furlough, was owned by a trust. Ruth was able to arrange a mortgage on it so that she would have a home to retire to when the time came. On her last furlough in the autumn of 2016, she began to update it, working on the garage (to make secure storage for gifts for Angola) and the front porch. It was a small project, but not without its problems. She'd fallen out with the builders, and as a result was left with a six- to seven-inch trench at the entrance to the porch. Each time she entered or left the house, she had to be careful stepping over the gap to avoid an accident. It was a constant reminder of her extra 'career' as a supervisor on the many building projects she'd had responsibility for in Angola. There had been plenty of arguments with labourers and with officials and a myriad of other problems, all much more significant than a wee trench at her front door.

Aside from driving, her involvement in building projects began in the mid-nineties, when she and Mary were both living in Saurimo. Neither had any experience of construction, but there was a need for a building to house a medical clinic and also one to serve as an office for the Emmaus work. In the absence of anyone else, they had to knuckle down to the new challenge. It was a role which became a large part of Ruth's ministry later on, particularly in relation to schools, so these first two buildings were a kind of apprenticeship for much bigger projects. They also served to keep Ruth busy and helped to stop her fretting while, because of the restrictions on travel, she couldn't get out to the villages to work with women and children.

Building in Angola was in total contrast to building in the West. It is so easy for us to order ready-made bricks and cement and sand for mortar from the builder's merchants. (Or at least it was pre-pandemic and pre-Brexit.) There, the bricks had to be hand-made and preferably burnt, after first cutting large quantities of wood for the firing. It was very labour-intensive and the availability of wood became increasingly difficult as the war progressed. Huge swathes of the countryside, if not actually denuded of trees, were likely to be heavily mined. In Lunda Sul province most building materials, with the exception of sand, had to be flown in from Luanda. Building was only possible in the dry season. It was impossible to make and fire bricks outdoors in the rain, so in order to ensure they could make as much use of the dry season as possible, locals built a shelter to enable the brick-making process for the clinic and office to be started in advance. Aside from making bricks they had to collect stones for the foundations. Many in the West have the mistaken idea that in countries like Angola you just decide to build something and start – without the trials of planning permission and building control. On privately owned land on a mission station that was possible, but otherwise there was a lot of red tape and hoops to be jumped through. For Ruth and Mary, working well outside their comfort zone, dealing with government officials was an additional pressure on top of the basic problems of designing the buildings, organising the materials and overseeing the building work itself.

However, by June 1997 the foundations for both buildings were in and several thousand bricks made, ready for burning. Ruth was in Luanda on her way home to England on furlough and took the opportunity to purchase cement, roofing sheets and all the doors and windows before she left. Forget B&Q – this wasn't a straightforward task, and as well as sourcing the materials, she needed to organise the transport to get them to Saurimo. This was expensive even in peacetime, and the war made it extremely difficult to arrange as well as costly. By autumn the basic structure was 'finished', but it still needed the plumbing and electrical installation, and for that they hoped to have an experienced volunteer workforce from the UK. Several times, despite the war, individual volunteers or teams came out to help with building projects. The renovation of the mission house at Camundambala was particularly welcome. It included underpinning, as the walls were beginning to crack, undertaken by a 'Brass Tacks' team – a Christian organisation dedicated to supporting missionaries through practical help.

Four years on, looking ahead to the possibility of peace and a resumption of travel, Brian, by now a resident missionary, oversaw the construction of a dormitory on the Emmaus Bible School site in Saurimo. It was for short residential courses for elders, Sunday school teachers and literacy motivators. A room to house the Risograph for printing course booklets was built on the same site. Ruth, released from the need to oversee the building project, was still needed to transport sand and stones in her vehicle, and to source cement, electrical wiring, plumbing materials and roofing sheets in Luanda. Most materials were now available, at a price. The main issue in getting them up from the capital was also the cost. It was a five-day drive each way, and even with their own truck, the fuel, the drivers' salaries, and bed and breakfast and food for them en route, came to around £1,000. This time the local volunteers made several thousand cement blocks, with the expectation that the buildings would be much more durable.

Between 2003 and 2016, when Debbie and the children were back in the UK for their boys' education, Brian came back and forwards for several months at a time to supervise building projects and to preach and teach in the churches and run Bible studies and seminars for groups of youths and men. Ruth looked forward to his visits, but in between she carried on facilitating, supporting and supervising building work. She was aware of how vital the building work was but also conscious that, even when Brian was in charge, her part in it sapped her strength and energy. And when on her own, she didn't find it easy to 'pace herself' physically, nor to determine how much of her time she should devote to it.

The work was financed by funds from the UK. Sometimes it was paid for out of money that was intended for Ruth's personal support; at other times there were gifts sent specifically for building projects. In 2006 Ruth received a legacy gift of £5,000. With peace holding, she was keen to re-establish the mission station at Biula as a base for reaching out to the villages around it, and to provide suitable accommodation for visiting preachers. Unusually, especially in an area that had been on a 'front line' in the conflict, the mission station buildings hadn't been totally destroyed, but they had been looted, with windows and doors and internal fittings stolen. With the gift she was able to put proper windows and inner doors into the old Wiseman house, paint the interior walls, and cement the floors at Biula school.

It wasn't all plain sailing. When the building of a medical clinic at Chapoji was finished, Ruth had a run-in with the government inspectors. When they declared it wasn't up to standard, Ruth, extremely irritated, informed them, 'You should be glad if someone qualified was giving out medicines under a tree!' It maybe wasn't the wisest of responses, and perhaps (though it's unlikely) a more conciliatory answer might have produced a different result. As it was, the roof had to be taken off and redone, and some internal divisions altered. It was annoying, time-consuming and an expense she could have done without, and made her thankful for the remoteness of Biula and Luma, where inspections were rare. Maybe you think a missionary should be capable of containing their frustrations and deal more gently with people and attitudes that are difficult. But they are just as human as the rest of us, and her reaction was understandable on several counts. At this point she was once again on her own, and therefore particularly tired. She was also frustrated, as one of the inspectors was the head of the government medical work in Saurimo, with whom she had regular contact, so he could easily have told her much earlier in the process that the plan needed to be altered.

The repair work on the houses and clinic at Biula was ongoing, as was the building of a store and a little house at Luma. It was intended to double as somewhere for Ruth to stay when she was down there, and also provide accommodation for visiting preachers. Originally, when peace came, the villagers built her a little mud hut – but it only had mud floors and an outside pit latrine at quite a distance from the house, which might, in Ruth's words 'prove a challenge to a visitor!' Five years on, it was badly cracked and needed major repairs, so it made sense to replace it with a more durable house, which ideally would have a bathroom. Distance was making this slow, but she was taking down materials when she could. She wanted to spend more time at Luma, especially to encourage the local Christians who had burnt 10,000 bricks for her, but it was tricky to find the time to take workers there and get them organised. The travel was horrendous – the road to Biula very muddy where the tarmac had broken up and the road into Luma a deep lake in places. Only a Land Rover could get through.

Various building projects continued throughout the remainder of her time, sometimes with outside help, sometimes on her own. At Biula, they varied from extensions and renovations, in the case of two of the houses, to the complete replacement of the church. The larger or more complicated projects were left until either Brian or Jonathan were out; simpler stages could be overseen by Ruth.

For the new church she transported twenty tons of stone from an old disused quarry to make the foundations, and then began to build up a stock of cement, taking some down in the back of the Land Rover every time she visited. On a single trip Jonathan and another volunteer from Scotland made 4,500 bricks for the walls and also put in ceilings in the old Wiseman house. The villagers were delighted to see the church up to roof level, and much more pragmatic than Ruth when there had to be a delay in putting on the roof, as Jonathan had to be fitted with a pacemaker, so couldn't return as quickly as he'd hoped.

Eventually, the church was finished, a water tank installed in the village and the water from the ram pumped into the Wiseman house. A new missionary family based themselves in the Wiseman house but felt they needed an extension to provide more bedroom and study space for the children. They found the prospect daunting, as the price of ballast and crushed stone was nearly double what they'd have had to pay in Saurimo. As a first step, the bathroom was enlarged to provide a shower, part of the veranda incorporated into a bedroom, and the bowed roof timbers sorted. When, in 2015, another missionary family also decided to base themselves at Biula, Ruth set about renovating a house for them. All the cracks were repaired, and the walls painted, covering up all the graffiti that dated from the war. Ceilings were installed throughout and Ruth herself wired the house to give lights in each room and sockets in the kitchen and lounge. She was somewhat concerned that it really needed to be fully wired by a qualified electrician, especially in a house with children, but for the time being it had to do. It was yet another skill that Ruth had learnt out of necessity and which she had never dreamt before she went to Angola would be part of her missionary work. The final task was to get the remaining windows, as there were still some gaps with just burglar bars, which were the greater priority.

Things didn't always turn out as expected. A machine for making blocks, which seemed like a good idea at the time, turned out to be a white elephant. Ruth found out about its existence when she was buying blocks for building, rather than getting the Angolans to make them using a mould. It should have been quicker, and easier, to buy them, however, the supply wasn't reliable. At one point, having paid for 5,000 blocks, she was still waiting months later for 3,000 of them, as the supplier couldn't keep up with demand. She thought the machine would be a great buy, not only to improve the build quality, but also had the potential to start a micro industry, providing employment, as well as generating funds for the missionary work. Sadly, a year later the Chinese arrived in Saurimo, making it cheaper and more efficient to buy cement blocks from them. (If anyone has a use for a machine for making blocks, it's still sitting at Camundambala – free to a good home!)

Chapter Seventeen

'Ngunaliumbu longesenu ana jetu'
'Please teach our children'

Cornwall, 2017

There were several primary schools close to Ruth's house, and standing at the kitchen sink it was just possible to see the roof of one of them, poking up beyond the neighbour's garden. At break and lunchtimes she could hear the children playing in the playground. It was a poignant reminder of 'her' schools in Angola.

Angola: School work

Constructing, equipping and running four schools, with varying success, in Lunda Sul province became a major part of Ruth's work from 2002 onwards. Despite her teaching background, it hadn't been her main aim when she first arrived. But in a country that had suffered nearly forty years of conflict, with the decimation of the education system, where it had existed at all, schools were a priority.

It was in 2000, with the hope of a move towards peace, that she was first asked to set up a school. This was a government request for a school in the refugee camp at Dala. The first task had been to erect a school 'building' of grass mats for walls and tree trunks for seats. That was the responsibility of the refugees themselves. She had enough pencils and exercise books to start at the beginning of the official school year, which in Angola at that time was in February. As the government was to pay the teachers, Ruth's prayer had been that they would be committed to regular attendance (unusual in government schools) and to teaching the '3Rs'. She hoped to take the opportunity to communicate the love of Christ to the children. If peace truly came, literacy would be the first step for many to enable them to make a living, but, most importantly for Ruth, it would enable them to read the Bible for themselves.

The Dala refugee school provided the first two years of schooling, and each year had four classes, with between forty-three and eighty-nine children in each. (Not much opportunity for individual learning plans there!) As well as the children who could get a seat on the tree trunks, others crammed in and sat on tins, while still others who couldn't fit inside listened from outside. In true 'Angolan time' fashion, the children drifted in at different times, which made it difficult for the teachers. Aside from the government-paid teachers, there were two whom Ruth paid for that were members of the church in the camp. They were more regular in attendance than their government-paid colleagues and the children in the classes taught by the two Christian teachers did much better in their exams than those in the other classes. The result was that everyone clamoured to be in the Christian teachers' classes. While Ruth appreciated their dedication, she feared it might lead to pressure on them to accept bribes, from those who could afford them, to take their children into their classes, so prayed they would withstand the temptation.

The desperate need at Dala was replicated across the country, and crystallised for Ruth the need for modern missionaries to get involved in education, as years earlier the pioneering missionaries had done. Then it had been to establish schools for the first time, now it would be to repair the damage done by war. It needed both time and resources. And just as when she had first heard God's call, when Angolan Christians in Lunda Sul pleaded with her to build schools for their children, that same inner voice prompted her to accept the task. She had the skillset and experience to run a school and, although she had been a secondary school teacher in the UK and these schools would provide primary education, developing a curriculum based on government guidelines was also well within her capabilities. Overseeing their construction was a different matter entirely.

There were three obvious sites for permanent schools – at the previous mission stations of Biula and Luma Cassai, and at Camundambala, where

Brian and Debbie were stationed. At Luma it was a case of renovating the building, while at Biula it needed to be built from scratch. By 2005, the school at Luma was functioning, though still needing some final touches, including windows and paint. Three of the four teachers were working well and an elder from the church fellowship went in each week to give Bible lessons to the children. Biula hadn't been so straightforward. Ruth had said she would help by providing roofing sheets, furniture and school books if the village provided the labour. It resulted in a stand-off of almost a year, while the villagers waited to see if she would do it all for them. When she didn't cave in to the pressure, the whole village started working. She wrote – '*Typical Chokwe reaction – see how far they can push and then capitulate with good grace and work hard!*'

They made thousands of mud bricks and got the three classrooms up to roof level.

The cost from the government for stones and gravel for the cement floors was prohibitive, so the local people gathered stones into heaps to be transported to the school via the mission lorry. When the lorry crashed, it caused a temporary halt, but in the meantime, doors and windows were welded ready to be taken down.

At Camundambala, Brian and Ruth also said they would pay for materials and the village would have to provide the labour. And as at Biula there was a long stand-off and then a sudden capitulation. The building work started and was going well, but the rainy season was approaching, so to move things on Ruth decided to bring down some workers from Saurimo to help. Instead of helping, it led to the Camundambala men downing tools. No unions there, but clearly bringing in 'outsiders' even from only ten kilometres away caused offence. Three weeks later, after Ruth pulled the Saurimo men out and when it was clear she wasn't bringing them back, the Camundambala men restarted. Unfortunately, the rains had come, causing one wall to collapse, so it needed to be rebuilt. Though they did manage to get the roof on, the delay meant no classrooms would be ready for the official start of the school year in February, and further work would have to wait for the dry season. That gave Ruth time to work on expanding the government curriculum to include Bible teaching and to develop teaching plans to ensure it wouldn't simply be rote learning, as was the norm in government schools.

The three schools took up a lot of time, energy and money, but her twin prayers were that it would produce a literate generation and that the claims of Christ could be presented to the children and lead to many finding a living faith.

In February 2007, Camundambala school finally opened after complaints from the authorities that there wasn't a dedicated library, not enough windows and the chairs were too small! Considering most villages had nothing, while in the towns children had to bring their own chair to school, Ruth thought it a bit much. But the parents and kids were delighted, which was what really counted. However, the official opening went well. Ruth wasn't into 'ribbon-cutting' ceremonies, but it was important to local folk as it got them on national TV. It was also a chance to let the government see what had been done. After the negativity she'd had from lesser officials, Ruth was pleased, not only to find the top two men were really impressed, but, unusually, to receive a 'thank you'.

As a result of Jonathan Singleton's input, the build was of a higher quality than it would otherwise have been. Left to herself Ruth wouldn't have bothered with ceilings, but with Jonathan and others able to install them they did so. Of course, it also increased costs, but she admitted it made a much better job and was more practical. Each class could be taught without hearing what was being said in the next room. Basic materials, such as stationery and pencils, were a priority, and she wanted to have class sets of reading books, so that there could be one per desk (if not per child). But there were also extras she hoped to get over time – a store for garden tools and sports equipment and an area for the kids to play basketball.

There were three classrooms functioning, and as it was just ten kilometres out of town, Ruth was 'hands on'. She was teaching two classes herself initially, until the government provided six teachers, three for the morning and three for the afternoon, leaving her free to supervise. The reception class had sixty children who had never held a pencil or sat on a chair and spoke no Portuguese, which was the official language for schools, so it was a tough job for the teacher. She would have liked to split the class, but she didn't feel she should, in case she wasn't able to maintain it all year, so instead she helped out when she could, even if it was just for half a day. One issue that Ruth hadn't anticipated was how pungent it would be having sixty children in one room under a metal roof in the Angolan sun. The teachers attempted to minimise the problem by lining them all up at the beginning of the day and sending away any who hadn't washed.

Most teachers were teaching half of the day and studying themselves in the other half. They had little or no understanding of good teaching practices and often focused on rote learning for those who couldn't read, and getting those who could to copy word for word what was in the textbooks or on the blackboard. As a result, Ruth planned to provide training herself. She was, however, delighted with their commitment, as it was rare in government schools for teachers to turn up every day. Even the children clapped and cheered when the teachers arrived each morning. Not the reaction that would be expected in the UK.

It still needed a toilet block, as the kids were having to go into the bush or use the latrines behind the church. But the need for another classroom was more urgent, so she halted the work on the toilets in order to renovate an existing building into a classroom.

Both Biula and Luma schools were also functioning, but not at full capacity. The main problem in each case was the rural location. Luma had a lovely Christian teacher for reception and first and second classes. But they were unable to run third and fourth classes due to a lack of teachers. Most wanted to remain in towns where they could teach and finish their own education as well. Even of those who were qualified, few were willing to go to rural areas without TV, telephones, secondary schools or doctors. Just one class was functioning at Biula with a government teacher. Ruth felt that what was most needed was a Christian who'd be willing to relocate to run the school. She decided to pay for a man who, though a good teacher and a Christian, was too old to be considered for the government payroll.

To begin with, Ruth tried to visit both Luma and Biula every month, but often it stretched to six weeks, and as the road continued to deteriorate, she couldn't do much more than support them with books, pencils, and chalk.

There were significant stresses and challenges of overseeing the building of the three schools simultaneously along with developing the curriculum and the general running of Camundambala. So Ruth was very grateful for the help of two primary-trained teachers from the UK, who came out for a short period. They improved classroom methods, produced a workbook for the reception class, and helped in the day-to-day running of the school. Towards the end of the school year all the teachers at Camundambala, bar one, had made good progress and gained confidence in their teaching skills, which was a great start.

Aware that she needed a break, Ruth planned to take a quick trip home in September for her brother's wedding. She needed to be back in time for the end of year exams in October and November to ensure there was no corruption in pupil pass rates and to oversee the registration of the children for the following school year. She wanted to ensure that all new pupils were from the villages and not from well-to-do families in Saurimo. A school that functioned every day and had good facilities was attractive to government dignitaries and elders in the town churches. She was concerned that they'd be willing to pay the teachers to admit their kids. Her plan for Camundambala in the incoming year was to build three more classrooms and the toilet block and, having sorted out a curriculum for reception and year one, organise the curriculum for year two. The school building was eventually finished and fully functioning in 2009. It had been a long project, but it was recognised as the best school in the area.

As the schools work progressed, it took up more and more of Ruth's time and energy. Sometimes things went very well and she was encouraged. At other times staff were either unreliable or placed under severe pressure due to personal and family problems. There was a constant need for more teachers who were both competent and reliable, as often those the government supplied were neither. At one point she was short of four teachers at Camundambala so had to teach morning and afternoon each day. She struggled to cope with that, as well as run the school, plus all the other demands on her time. One of the teachers who spoke to me talked of Ruth going out at lunchtime and coming back wearing a fresh blouse, but which, because of the rush, she'd managed to put on inside out without noticing.

The last school Ruth opened was a 'junior' primary school, in the village of Kwasamukwenu, fifteen kilometres away, so that the forty children under the age of nine who currently attended Camundambala could have their first four years of education in their own village. Previously, those who hadn't any relatives with whom they could stay during the week had walked in and out on a narrow dust track every day. Contrast that with the maximum two miles that young primary children can be expected to walk in the UK. Any further and the government provides free transport. Initially Ruth taught reception and year one herself, as the teacher the government supplied had no intention of teaching but was happy to take a salary for doing nothing. Eventually, Ruth, fed up with his unreliability, told him to 'Start his own school and not try to *take over ours'* and employed another person herself. In Angola, in the last two years of schooling each person must choose between the nursing 'stream' or the teaching 'stream'. Anyone who has finished year ten can teach, but they need to apply to get 'teacher' status. This (as usual) often led to corruption – people who wanted to be on the government payroll bribed those who made the decisions. Ruth, who refused to bribe anyone, prayed that the teacher she'd employed would get teacher status without bribery.

There were many times in Ruth's last four years when she had to employ and pay for teaching staff out of her own support budget, otherwise the schools wouldn't have been able to continue to function. There were moments of encouragement – for example when the director of education in Lunda Sul promised help to pay teachers of Ruth's choice for the school at Kwasamukwenu. It was the first time in fourteen years she'd had such positive interest shown by the government, but despite the promises, the payment for two community teachers didn't materialise.

In January 2015 the government agreed to an amalgamation of the mission school at Camundambala with the government primary at the main road end. It released the government school building for years seven to nine, avoiding the need for young teenagers to travel into Saurimo until their final year.

She expected the amalgamation to be challenging, but it stretched her beyond anything she could have imagined. She was promised six of the eight government teachers, but only three turned up. And as she got the pupils' files, she realised they were enrolling many more pupils than the government school had the previous year. When, surprise, surprise, she found money in two files, she suspended enrolments while she checked the situation. It was a shock to find that the government's ninety-eight children on the books for the previous year had grown to two hundred. It stretched both resources and space, so she had had to use the two classrooms in the adjacent leprosy village and still had over fifty children in year one. It was even more concerning when she started covering for teachers who didn't turn up. There were pupils in years five and six who couldn't even write their names properly, far less read and write. As a result, she decided to move all the government schoolchildren in years two and three back into year one and the fours to sixes into special literacy classes.

It was a challenging year in other ways too – there was an extra month's holiday in May for a national census, and again in August as Saurimo hosted the national schools' games. The net result was that few classes finished the curriculum, and even though the government announced that schools would continue till mid-December, most of the teachers gave up teaching, and some didn't even attend after the end of October when holidays normally begin. With some short-term help Ruth did the assessment of years one and two and brought pupils in for extra teaching in maths and reading, but still more than the usual number of kids had to repeat.

The previous year Ruth had run a seminar for the teachers in reception and year one in all six primary schools in the area around Camundambala. The 'norm' for teaching was to fill the blackboard and tell the pupils to copy it, and then stand on the veranda chatting to colleagues or making phone calls. Interaction with the pupils and marking their work was foreign to them. She was pleased to note, in what was to be her final year in Angola, that the amalgamation of the schools at Camundambala was settling down, with the government teachers *'beginning to get the hang of teaching!'*

In order to encourage the children she gave small prizes to those who worked hard and tried their best, but Ruth also wanted the children to have fun, and so she organised football championships and introduced another innovation which she called the 'Day of the Child'. This Angolan version of a primary school 'sports day' took place at the end of the school year. And just as in the UK, alongside the normal races, there were novelty races, such as a sack race and games such as ducking for lollipops in a bucket of manioc flour and making a slide out of tarpaulin and fairy liquid.

Kwasamukwenu school was also running well, with two teachers paid for by Ruth and three by the government. Ruth was also still paying for Christian teachers at Luma but had applied for funding from the government for them. Aside from releasing funds for other mission work, there was one very important practical reason why it was better to have all the teachers paid by the government. If the mission paid for a teacher, it wasn't only the teaching that needed to be adequate but also their personal life and reputation, otherwise the reputation of the mission would also suffer. Therefore, a person paid by the mission, who was a good teacher but who was found to be committing adultery or stealing, for example, would have to be sacked – potentially leaving a class with no teacher. As government employees, their personal and professional life could remain separate, unless it actually impacted on the children or their ability to fulfil their role. As mission employees it couldn't.

Initiatives begun with great hopes aren't always successful, and one of the 'failures' was the school at Biula. Defeated by distance, by the impossibility of being able to supervise adequately, and by the lack of good teachers, when the school building itself began to fall down, Ruth had to let it go. It was sad for her to see it demolished, but the roofing sheets, too valuable to be thrown away or left to rust, were saved for future use.

At Camundambala, however, the school had now grown so much, in both numbers and reputation, that when that building also began to deteriorate, it was clear a new school was needed. There wasn't any realistic possibility of either local funding or expertise to replace it, and Ruth, though not knowing her time of service was coming to an end, recognised she had neither the energy nor the expertise to supervise the building of a new school, this time of more permanent construction. Instead, she sketched out a plan of what she felt was needed and passed the responsibility for implementing it to Brian Howden. The planning for the new school was, though neither of them knew it, the beginning of the process of 'handing on the baton' of the mission work in the whole area.

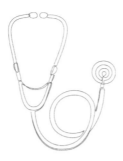

Chapter Eighteen

'Hingumanununa kuma kwana kwakuzomboka, hingunafungu ufulielo'
'I have finished the race, I have kept the faith'

Angola: Illness suspected

In December 2016, shortly after returning to Angola from furlough, Ruth discovered a hard mass in her breast. It was a shock, for she'd had a medical during the furlough and nothing of note had been found. Fortunately, Sam Simonyi-Gindele was currently at Biula and was able to advise her to go home to have it checked out. She'd planned a retreat for the Emmaus workers and a kid's camp for the first two weeks of January, and was looking forward to both of them, so it was decided the Emmaus retreat would go ahead without her, but the kid's camp would be postponed until the next school holiday. She arrived in the UK on Christmas Eve and was picked up at Heathrow by her brother and sister-in-law, Tim and Natalie, but hoped to be back in Angola soon.

Cornwall, 2017: Illness confirmed

On January 13th 2017, Ruth went to Treliske hospital for her oncology appointment. It was not good news. She had a very fast growing and aggressive breast cancer. She knew from the outset that the treatment was going to be tough and in the end the cancer would kill her, but she hoped she might get a period of remission that would allow her to go back to Angola one last time. More tests followed, and she began what were planned to be six cycles of chemotherapy, taking a total of eighteen weeks. After that there would be yet more tests and the possibility of surgery. She was keeping all those who prayed and supported her up to date with her situation, and wrote, 'I have felt a God-given peace today, but it will be a long and difficult road.' *She admitted to being fearful, not of dying, for that would be* 'going home to the Lord she loved', *but of the process along the way.*

Three weeks later the results of the bone scan brought more potentially bad news. It showed something 'suspicious' *in her pelvic area. To do the appropriate tests to find out exactly what it was would have put the chemotherapy regime back, and the doctors felt it was more important to proceed. The first step was a guided tour of the hospital department where she would spend increasing amounts of time over the next five months. Her chemotherapy was scheduled to start on the 15th February, with a hefty cocktail of three drugs. She had always kept her hair long, which meant that there wasn't an enormous difference between photos of her in her late twenties, when she first went to Angola, and those taken in her fifties. It was a wrench to cut it short in preparation for the treatment, but she hoped that when it started to fall out it wouldn't feel so dramatic.*

She made good use of the time before her first cycle of chemotherapy. Knowing that she wouldn't be going back to Angola any time soon, she emailed and phoned folk there to ensure that things she'd left undone due to her quick departure would be sorted. To relax she watched football on Sky Sports, happy to see any live matches. Her brother took her for days out – revisiting scenes from their childhood – driving around the Cornish coast to watch the sea and be drenched by sea spray on the cliffs, and visiting coves and beaches. They went tenpin bowling, which, true to form, she won with two strikes in a row. It was her last sporting achievement. There were a few trips further afield – to Exeter to see the underground passages which had been used as air raid shelters during the Blitz. They were a poignant reminder of hiding in her passageway in her house in Saurimo during a gun battle. In the Royal Albert Memorial Museum, the taxidermy exhibits included a giraffe, an elephant and a tiger. It amused her that in all her years in Africa she'd only seen these animals once – not in Angola, for, as a result of the war, there weren't any, but on a trip to Zambia.

She visited people who had supported her over the years, and lots of people visited her. Colleagues and fellow workers from Angola; trustees from Echoes of Service; and friends from her home church and further afield. To begin with she could make them tea, as she always would have done in the past, but gradually, due to increasing tiredness and the effect of the treatment, she had to allow others to make it for her. Her conversations centred around Angola, for though she was physically in Cornwall, her mind and her heart were still in Lunda Sul. One of her friends, who had also been out to visit (and to help), said that once Ruth started talking about Angola, she could hardly be stopped. She talked of the people, the locations, the work already done, and still to do.

On her birthday, amongst her presents, she was given the biography of an American missionary doctor who worked with Samaritan's Purse and had contracted Ebola. The title was Called for Life, *and Ruth read it in a day. She knew that she too had been called for life and that life was coming to an end. When she began to have problems sleeping, her brother made up a compilation of Christian hymns and instrumentals of hymn tunes from some of his CDs for her to listen to.*

It wasn't long before she was beginning to experience significant discomfort. By mid-February the tumour was beginning to break through her skin. Three times in eight days she had late-night trips to the accident and emergency department in Truro to get relief from the pain. The normal route from Ruth's house towards Truro went through roads with speed bumps. They were nothing to what she had driven over and through in Angola, scarcely bothering to slow down. It hadn't fazed her, though the car often suffered as a result. Now, however, her brother had to take an alternative route to avoid the bumps, because going over them, even slowly, gave her so much discomfort.

Her sister-in-law, Natalie, was her treatment 'buddy', going to all her hospital appointments with her and supporting her throughout her last months. Her first chemotherapy week was tough, but much as expected. She got up to have breakfast with her tablets, then needed another hour or so in bed to gather enough strength to shower and dress. It took a frustratingly long time, and Ruth wasn't used to having to move slowly. In the seven days following the infusion she felt progressively more tired and less able to concentrate. The second week was better, and the third week, leading up to the next dose, was the best of the three.

Her second cycle began well, with new anti-emetics, but with the third infusion her pain levels went through the roof. The protocol for pain relief was neither a quick nor an easy fix. First, she was given paracetamol and ibuprofen, followed by a wait to see if they worked. Then co-codamol and another wait. Then oral morphine and wait again. Six hours and a lot of pain later, Ruth was finally taken into A & E and put on an IV morphine drip. After a night in the hospital, she went home, with slow-release morphine to try to control the pain. She had several good days during that three-week cycle, when she was able to eat a meal, but others when she was totally floored, with no energy or strength. The breast pain continued throughout. She was still happy to have visitors, though, as long as they didn't come too early in the morning, would knock and let themselves in, give her time to put on her wig, not be put off or panic if she retched, and understand if sometimes she wasn't up to much on any given day.

On the 17th April, Easter Monday, two weeks after her third cycle of chemotherapy, she had a day out, visiting Helston Heritage Railway. A high point of that trip was the ride in the guard's van. It was to be the last time she left the house other than to go to hospital. One month later she was admitted with low blood pressure and nausea and put on a drip. She had been carried from the house to the ambulance in a chair, and as she left, she looked back at her lounge and said, 'You know I may not be coming home.' Afterwards, her brother went into her bedroom and found the CD player paused on a Len Magee song about heaven. It was the last song she heard.

At first the doctor discussed surgery with her – an operation that could take anything from one and a half hours just to close the wound, to eight hours if they could remove the tumour. She was bright and chatty, despite the pain, and appreciated the visits of a nurse who came to pray with her on her breaks. She also tried to keep in touch with all her family and close friends. But over the next month the tumour continued to grow, despite the chemotherapy, and it became clear surgery was not an option. The new plan was for six weeks of radiotherapy and then possibly more chemotherapy after that.

She moved to the hospice, because they could provide better treatment for the side effects of the radiotherapy. By the time they moved her she couldn't concentrate to read any longer, but just before she left the hospital, she told her brother she'd been reading Psalm 116 and it had given her great comfort. It includes the verse, 'Precious in the sight of the Lord is the death of his faithful servant.[13] *He knew then she'd begun to look up, not back, and was ready to go.*

---

13 Psalm 116 v 15

The doctors were still proposing more treatment, but Ruth refused. Brian and Debbie were among the last of her non-family visitors. They came on the 5th and 6th July and had a long conversation about the work in Angola. She didn't try to tell them what they should do. Instead, she said it was God's timing for the work to pass into their hands and she was at peace. Talking to her brother, in what was to be one of her last conversations, she spoke of the legacy she felt she was leaving to Angola. Missionary work in previous times had been done 'to' the Angolans. Now, in Brian and Debbie's hands, it would be done 'with' them. As she fell sleep for the last time, before she lapsed into unconsciousness, she was humming hymn tunes quietly to herself. For the whole of her last week, she had family with her. Some were there all day and only went home to sleep; one brother remained through the nights, sleeping in a reclining chair beside her bed. He slipped away for a shower each day when others were with her. She was comfortable and free from pain and without any signs of agitation as she waited to be 'called home'. Half an hour before she died, the family all witnessed something very strange. As they sat around Ruth's bed, they became aware of the very distinctive smell of the cooking fires from an Angolan bush village. Tim, Natalie and Phil had all visited Ruth and therefore recognised the smell. Tim got up to look out the window to see if a hospice groundsman was burning garden clippings. But there was no fire, and when he opened the window, they discovered the smell was only in the room. They tried the corridor but it wasn't there either. There was no rational explanation and none of the family were prone to fanciful ideas. All they could say was – the smell was real; it was in the room, and they all smelt it. Ruth had always hoped she would get back to Angola to say her last goodbyes, but that hadn't been possible. But it was as if God had brought Angola to her, through the scent of an African cooking fire.

Ruth Hadley passed peacefully into glory on the 19th July 2017, with family by her side. She was sixty-one years old and had served God in Angola for over thirty-four years. Her journey through Angola had been long and difficult, but over and over again she had experienced the faithfulness of God. Towards the end of her service, she wrote:

> *It is so good to look back and see God's faithfulness in so many different circumstances. There have been times of great challenge, of great joy, of disillusionment, of sheer fear and of great sorrow,*

especially during the war years. I am reminded of the clarion call to 'make disciples' [14] *but I do not know how I would cope each day if it were not for God's sustaining grace. It is a privilege to serve him in this land.*

As she relied on the faithfulness of God, so, in the words carved on her headstone, she has received His commendation: 'Well done, good and faithful servant.'[15]

---

14 Matthew ch 28 v 19

15 Matthew ch 25 v 21

Afterword

In Angola, and particularly in Lunda Sul province there was an outpouring of grief, following the news of her death. Óbitos (wakes) were held in various places, including at the Emmaus office site and the church fellowship that Ruth attended in Saurimo. The óbitos in Saurimo lasted for several days, with three to four hundred people at each one. They carried on with their daily work, but came together each evening and remained throughout each night singing hymns. At Biula, where Ruth had begun her missionary service, around two hundred women gathered for two days to read the Bible and to sing hymns. The scale of the óbitos indicated the love, respect and gratitude the Chokwe Christians had for Ruth.

Her funeral was held in St Austell on 11th August 2017. The simple grave-side service was followed in the afternoon by a Thanksgiving service attended by several hundred people. It was live-streamed and watched online by around one thousand people in Zambia, DR Congo, Canada, USA, Spain, Sweden, Eire, Northern Ireland, Scotland, England and Wales.

The three-hour long service, led by Ken Rudge, an elder in Ruth's home church, included tributes from family, friends, missionary colleagues and the Angolan church representatives. The tributes were illustrated with photographs, slides and videos and interspersed with hymns which reflected Ruth's life and work. Although a sad occasion, it was also a celebration of all that God had accomplished through her.

Acknowledgments

I am grateful for the many people who contributed to the writing of this book. Those who shared their memories of Ruth with me, both in person and via zoom in the UK and in Angola are listed in the Appendix – I hope I haven't left anyone out, if I have, I'm truly sorry.

Special thanks must go to Ruth's brothers and to those who generously offered me hospitality as I travelled around the UK interviewing folk, at a time when, due to covid 19, people thought very carefully about having visitors - Ken and Della Rudge, Jonathan and Ruth Singleton, John and Pearl Aitken and Johnny and Susan Ramsey.

I could not have carried this project through to completion without the help and support of Brian and Debbie Howden, who not only hosted me at Camundambala, drove me around Lunda Sul, organised interviews and translated for me; but were constantly at the end of 'WhatsApp' messaging both before and after my visit and while I was writing, to answer my many questions. Brian also provided the Chokwe translations of the phrases that appear at the start of each chapter. Finally, I must thank Echoes International, who initiated this project, and gave me access to the letters Ruth wrote home during her years in Angola, on which much of this narrative is based.

Appendix

Those who shared their memories of Ruth and helped to make the book possible.

In Angola

Issac Buca, Kaluji, the elders and deacons at Viana church, Jorge, José Neto, Philip, Massone, Horano, Lucas, Bijel, Chisseque, Chipoia, Teófilo, Nazare, Marcus, Anita, Mavunda, Chavuma, Andre, Arménia, Paula, José Sachombo, Estevão, Lucia, Korindu, Sam Simonyi-Gindele, Sergio, Justo, Mario, Oscar, Sampaio, Lilli, Esau, Afonso, Zebedeu, Marcus Donji, Eliseu, Isabel, Irene, Jacob, Matus, Pedro and Albertina, Kamawe, Lenguela, Carlito, Victorino, Ferreira, Kayleigh and Joel Griffen, Brian and Debbie Howden.

In the UK

Phil Hadley, Stephen Hadley, Tim Hadley, Ken and Della Rudge, Bill Evans, Sue and Colin Hares, Geoff and Sue Fox, Bryan and Margaret Charles, Stuart and Jenny Dan, Paul and Ann Roberts, Jen Ashley, Jonathan and Ruth Singleton, Johnny and Susan Ramsey, Bebe Cadman, Paul and Angie Law, Adrian French, Ken Barrett, Deborah Grigg, Alan Park, Victor Boyd, Eric and Margaret McCaughren, Iris Floyd, Derek Powell.

Abbreviations

IEIA	Brethren church in Angola
LWF	Lutheran World Federation
MAF	Mission Aviation Fellowship
MPLA	People's Movement for the Liberation of Angola
UN	United Nations
UNAVEM	United Nations Angola Verification Mission
UNICEF	United Nations Children's Fund
UNITA	National Union for the Total Independence of Angola
WPF	World Food Programme